For Sir Michael and Lady Oppenheimer

RICHARD BURTON
THE INDIAN MAKING OF AN ARABIST

Burton Memorial Lecture 1999

with best wishes from
SIMON DIGBY

D1391028

ORIENT MONOGRAPHS
JERSEY
2006

Richard Burton
The Indian Making of
an Arabist

First published 2006

by Orient Monographs

Jersey

ISBN 0 903971 02 X

Produced and distributed by
Melisende Publishing Ltd
Pennine Way Office
87-89 Saffron Hill
London EC1N 8QU
www. melisende.com

Edited by Leonard Harrow
Printed and bound in England at the St Edmundsbury Press

FOREWORD

The Sir Richard Burton medal is intended to commemorate the 19th century British traveller, scholar and translator. In the aftermath of the 1914-1918 war the Council of the Royal Asiatic Society had in 1919 decided to establish a formal lecture in Burton's name. In 1923 proposals were approved to bestow a medal upon the invited speaker. It is a handsome silver-gilt medal with a striking bust of Sir Richard Burton on the obverse, of which the stock of blanks and the reverse was held on behalf of the Society by the veteran numismatists, Messrs Spink and Co of London.

StJohn Philby was the first holder of the medal and among his successors was Freya Stark. Both of them like Burton were the authors of outstanding narratives of travels in the Arabian peninsula. Half a century later the classic age of British and west European travellers in the Middle East had become invested with the aura of a distant past.

This situation was recognized by the last award of the medal in 1978 to Dr W G Archer. Like Burton, Archer was interpreter and publicizer. He had brought knowledge and appreciation of aspects of the visual arts of India to a wide English reading public. In his earlier career in the Indian Civil Service before Independence, he had also done fieldwork in collecting rustic songs and bringing to the attention of a modern public the art of Indian tribal peoples. Archer, however, perhaps felt that he had nothing to say about Burton, and confined himself to lecturing within one of his chosen fields, upon the Kotah school of Rajput painting.

In 1999 the Council of the Royal Asiatic Society of Great Britain and Ireland decided to offer me their award of the Sir Richard Burton medal. It was intimated to me that in return I would be expected to deliver a talk celebrating some aspect of the great man's life and achievements.

It is now five years since I prepared this essay, which is a survey of Richard Burton's evolution into an 'Arabist' and 'Arabophile'. From one point of view the present paper is a commissioned work that I would

3

not have undertaken if I had not received an invitation to write on a topic related to Burton's life and work. Yet I felt competent to undertake this survey on account of my own exploration of aspects of the pre-modern Islamic and Indian worlds combined with an enduring interest in the structures of power of British rule in India in the colonial period. Moreover the proposed award was within the gift of an old British learned society, whose interests I had endeavoured to serve for more than a decade of my life by a long and chequered fight for the preservation and conservation of its historic collections.

Accordingly I have attempted to describe the course of the development of Burton's interests and abilities before he achieved fame from his account of his pilgrimage to Mecca. Some of Burton's attitudes and aptitudes were already moulded by what has been described as his 'desultory boyhood,' – that is to say his peculiar upbringing in a minor British gentry-class family, resident 'on the Continent' /of southern Europe/ in the early nineteenth century. On this was overlaid the experience and opportunities of seven years as a young officer in a 'Native Infantry' regiment in western India, playing a part in the fabric of British colonial rule. It was almost entirely in India that he acquired a taste for 'things Arab', as well as some of the linguistic and social skills which enabled his subsequent travels, explorations and literary works.

British society today is certainly not liberated from social and generational tensions similar to those which I have tried to analyze in the formation of Richard Burton's character and attitudes. I doubt whether I have adequately fulfilled the rôle expected from the recipient of a commemorative medal. My expressions of opinion sometimes conflict with the traditional obligation 'to praise famous men' on a formal commemorative occasion, yet I would not like to ignore what I feel are darker and harsher aspects of Burton's life and character.

I remain grateful to the Council of the Royal Asiatic Society for bestowing on me the Sir Richard Burton Medal, and for prompting me to attempt a historical essay somewhat apart from my current fields of interest. My analysis of the mainsprings of Burton's behaviour reflects my training in the History Tripos of the University of Cambridge five decades ago, and I would like to recall the kindness and guidance of my teachers in those distant days, Jack Gallagher and T G P Spear. Behind them is the powerful shade of my schoolday tutor W L McElwee, still remembered as a military historian. He was himself a pupil of Sir

4

Lewis Namier, who in his day greatly changed perceptions of English social history.

I have in the last five years rephrased some of the text of *Richard Burton: the Indian Making of an Arabist*. As a 'period-piece' that reflects the circumstances in which it was commissioned in the last year of the second millennium, it seemed to me more appropriate to make it available in print close to its original discursive form rather than alter it for another framework of publication.

Simon Digby   *Jersey, C.I.*
July 2006   *Channel Islands*

CONTENTS

RICHARD BURTON
The Indian Making
of an Arabist

When I was told that the Council of the Royal Asiatic Society were thinking of bestowing the Sir Richard Burton medal upon me, I was also informed I would be expected to deliver a lecture on a topic relevant to his life and labours. My delight that a Society with which I have been connected through almost the whole of my adult life should wish to honour me was tempered by a feeling of panic. I was not a specialist in any of the fields on which Sir Richard Burton wrote so copiously. I had not much to say about Burton's life and work that would not be well known to at least some of my audience.

On reflection I felt what I could most usefully provide was an analytical account of the making and shaping of Burton as an Arabist and Arabophile by the experience and opportunities of his seven years as an Indian Army officer. To this I could not resist adding a comment on Indian influences upon two of the great cycles of travel in the *Arabian Nights*.

Indian elements in two travel-cycles of the Arabian Nights

When I chose an initial title of this talk, it was 'Between India and Arabia,' I had intended to allow myself scope to discuss some of the Indian aspects and elements of the *Arabian Nights*, the annotated translaton of which is perhaps Burton's weightiest scholarly achievement. In an earlier period there was much speculation about such Indian elements. Burton himself believed that much of Arabian magic was of Indian origin and was inclined to see Sufism as originally emanating from India. Ideas of dissemination from India have been academically unfashionable outside the subcontinent for some decades, and more energy and ingenuity – particularly on the part of Western orientalists – has gone into the study of the reception into India in ancient times of influences from the West.

Nevertheless, exempli gratia, I would like to draw attention to the Indian links, of different kinds, with two important cycles of travel in the *Nights*. The European literature on the *Nights* is vast, and I cannot say that no one has made these particular connections before. The first, inevitably, is with the *Voyages of Sindbad*, where other Indian influences have often previously been discerned. There appears to be a direct descent of the narrative structure of the Voyages of Sindbad from a cycle of travels that was included in the lost original *Brihatkatha* or 'Great Narrative.' This cycle of travel does not appear in the *Kathāsaritsāgara*, of which Penzer's annotated edition is designed to copy and match Burton's many-volumed edition of the *Arabian Nights*,[1] but it occurs in the Nepalese Sanskrit *Brihatkathālokasamgraha* studied by Felix Lacôte in the first three decades of last century, and translated into English as *The Story of Sānudāsa* by J.A.B. van Buitenen some fifty years ago. Neither of these scholars refer to the connection.[2]

Both cycles of voyage as we now have them are divided into seven episodes. Both have a merchant hero and relate his travels overseas and in distant lands; both start with the dissipation of the paternal fortune of the adventurer, and both end in the location where they began, with the hero reunited with his family. There are many other points of resemblance, but two correspondences appear to be decisive. The name of the hero of the *Brihatkatha* cycle is Sānudāsa, providing the Arabic name of Sindbād the Sailor (not of course of the other Sindbād of the *Sindibād-nāma* transmission). Moreover in the seventh and last episode of both cycles the hero brings back a lady whose mother is an aerial spirit, a *Gandharva* or a *Jinnī*.[3]

The second cycle of travel in the *Nights* that appears to have strong Indian connections is that of Prince Sayf al-Mulūk and Princess Badī' al- Jamāl, but the connections are Indo-Persian and from a much later period. Alone among the stories of the *Nights*, Sayf al-Mulūk appears to have enjoyed an independent existence in the eastern Persian world. Of the manuscripts of the main independent Persian prose version, some are identified as Indian and one was written at Bijapur in the seventeenth century.[4] Metrical versions are known in Eastern Turkish, Deccani (Dakanī), Panjabi, Pushto and Sindhi.[5]

The frame story appears in the 'Egyptian recension' texts of the *Nights*, but is lacking in the Pétis de la Croix/Mukhlis Isfahānī version of the same tale.[6] It has had the names corrupted by the Arab adaptor or copyists, to whom they meant nothing. The king is Mahmūd

b. Sebuktegin of Ghazni and the merchant Hasan is the Wazīr Khwāja [Ahmad b.] Hasan Maymandī, who in the 'mirror for princes' literature plays an admonitory and corrective role at Mahmūd's court. In the Indo-Persian version of the frame story Nahrwāla (Anhilwāra-Patan) is among the cities from which a relation of the tale is sought. A firm *terminus ante quem* for the tale is set by the Deccani version by the Golkonda court poet Ghawwāsī, dating from 1035/1626.[7] Other indications perhaps favour a date of composition not earlier than the fifteenth century.[8]

British Arabists made in India

In contemporary oriental studies there is often an uncomfortable gap between Middle Eastern Islamic studies, and Indian or Indological studies that concentrate on Sanskritic literature and culture and, in its broadest sense, the Hindu religious tradition. Anyone who has had contacts with western Arabists, or specialists in 'neo-Persian' literature must have encountered examples of a distaste among them for the alien and barely comprehensible traditions of the Indian subcontinent. This distaste sometimes extends to 19th and 20th century Indo-British scholarship. With my own scholarly interests setting me somewhat apart from both the Islamic Middle Eastern and Sanskritic camps, I attempt to survey here the influence of Burton's earlier Indian experience upon his subsequent behaviour and upon his writings on the Islamic Middle East.

For so many British orientalists of the eighteenth and nineteenth centuries the road to the Muslim Middle East was back from India, where they had employment and opportunities for learning which were not available in British universities. The actual processes of the training of these apparently independent scholars and writers are seldom closely considered when mention is made of them. Thus Robert Irwin, in his learned, judicious and entertaining *Companion to the Arabian Nights*, remarks about Captain Jonathan Scott – translator of some Indo-Persian historical works as well as of the *Arabian Nights* – 'like so many eighteenth century Englishmen [*sic*], /he picked up/ Arabic and Persian in India.'[9]

Burton and his biographers

For Richard Burton's early life we have hundreds of pages of first-person narrative in his fragments of autobiography and in his first travel books,

11

written in India. Burton's narratives detail the opportunities, the stages and the intermediaries by which and through whom he attained his impressively wide and sometimes deep knowledge of oriental languages, his equal knowledge of alien codes of behaviour and his competence in donning oriental costumes and acting oriental character-roles. These skills that he acquired while he was serving as an officer in a 'Native Infantry Regiment' in western India, were the groundwork for his grandest piece of rôle-playing, that of al-Hājj 'Abd Allah on the pilgrimage to Mecca and al-Madina. They also sustained his most extended scholarly achievement, his comprehensive, abundantly annotated translation of the *Arabian Nights*.[10]

Besides Burton's own writings, there is a vast biographical literature both on Burton and his wife, to which even now there are frequent additions and reworkings. His dying widow Isabel hurried into print with over 1200 pages, to be followed post haste by his niece Miss Stisted.[11] In 1998 Mary Lovell in *A Rage to Live* produced over 900 pages, of rather denser print than Lady Burton's volumes.[12] The last biography before that, Fawn M Brodie's *The Devil Drives* (1967/1971) became a Penguin paperback of 500 pages of small print [13]Another serious modern effort, Byron Farwell's *Burton* (1963), runs to 430 dense pages.[14] It is a feature of these biographies that they all begin with Burton's ancestry and birth and end with his death, and they have to deal with the great variety of environments through which Burton and his spouse passed. Among the other twentieth century narratives one may make an exception of the shorter account in Lesley Blanch's *The Wilder Shores of Love*, [1954], as she tried to depict Isabel Burton as one of four European nineteenth century women with a passionate impulse towards the Arab Orient.[15]

All of the later writers are fascinated with the career and character of Richard Burton. For their detail and opinions regarding the backgrounds within and against which Burton lived, worked and wrote, they are inclined to draw heavily on the reminiscences of Burton himself, and those of his wife and his niece. For their judgements of Burton's scholarship in his diverse fields of interest, the accuracy or otherwise of his record of events and the scholarly merit of his writings the biographers take much on trust. They have often been obliged to rely upon the opinions of others regarding the circumstances of life in the east. Curiously, I think that none of the recent biographers has asked for an opinion from the modernised inhabitants of the countries about which Burton wrote, though nowadays there are notable and sometimes strongly expressed contributions from Anglophone Arabs. None of the biographers has chosen to approach Burton as an individual within a web of time, class and environment, whose behaviour may be compared to, and contrasted with that of other individuals within the same or similar circumstances – predecessors, contemporaries or successors.

Burton's seven years in India: the parallel with Kipling

Burton arrived in India at the age of 21 in 1842 and left the country in 1849 in some disappointment with his employment – in his own words – 'after seven years ... working like a horse, volunteering for every bit of service, and qualifying myself for all contingencies.'[16] One may note the curious parallel with Rudyard Kipling, who, when even younger than Burton, spent his 'seven years hard' as a reporter in India, and continued to draw upon and refashion his Indian experience for decades afterwards. Both these young men, it might also appear, by their writings made British India too hot to hold them – Burton (at least according to the suspect account, examined below, that he provided in the *Terminal Essay* to his translation of the *Nights*) by his report on the boy-brothels of Karachi;[17] Kipling in circumstances that appear to have escaped the notice of some of his sharpest-eyed biographers.[18] Both men only made brief visits to India in the subsequent decades of their quite long lives. A similarity between her husband and Mr Rudyard Kipling had occurred to Burton's wife Isabel.[19] The consideration of the formative influences on Burton in his early adult years in India may alert us to wider problems of personality patterns, the assumed and discarded personae and self- identifications of people of alien descent accultured in Indian and Islamic settings.

Burton's family and upbringing

Let us recall the brief details of Burton's life. We can use the entry upon him in Buckland's *Dictionary of Indian Biography,* published in 1906. From the point of view of the administrators of British India, Burton's defects are succinctly and urbanely, but decisively, indicated in this entry:[20]

BURTON, SIR RICHARD
(1821-1890). Traveller, author and linguist; son of Colonel
J. Netterville Burton: born March 19, 1821: educated on
the continent without system, and was at Trinity College,

Oxford, for five terms from 1840; to India, 1842, in the Bombay Native Infantry: made himself proficient in Oriental languages and studied Muhammadan life and customs thoroughly, at Baroda and in the Sind Survey, ... translated the *Arabian Nights,* with a fullness of text and notes which laid bare his minute knowledge of oriental nature ... His wife accompanied him wherever possible in his appointments and travels: and wrote a life of him, which was corrected by another account.

Burton himself, his wife and niece provide details of his ancestry and immediate forebears. Lesley Blanch, always a sentimentalist, describes the family as being 'well-born but impoverished.'[21] Most of the family connections and traditions that Burton or his wife narrated are not improbable, but a descent from a natural son of Louis XIV by a lady of the Montmorency family will recall, to readers of Thackeray's *Vanity Fair*, the heroine Becky Sharp on her path of upward social mobility:[22]

'How Miss Sharp is awakened by my words,' /the younger
Pitt Crawley thought; but then/ ... 'her mother was a
Montmorency.'

Burton's modern American biographers sometimes loosely describe him as of Irish stock. The Irish constituent of Burton's ancestry was from the Anglo- or Scoto-Irish Protestant ascendancy, but his patrilineal descent in that land only stretches to his great-uncle's and grandfather's appointments to benefices in the [Anglican] Church of Ireland. His father was a good-looking military officer, married to a plain English county Miss, whose money was carefully tied-up so that he could not get his hands upon it. This, as Burton recognized, kept the family from destitution. The manner in which Burton's father obtained a commission at the beginning of the Napoleonic wars seems to have verged on sharp practice, and after an undistinguished military career he had been put on half-pay when he incurred the disapproval of the Duke of Wellington. The family spent much of its time on the Continent, possibly for financial reasons. In short this was a family like many others, from the raffish and insecure end of the non-mercantile British gentry class. As both Burton and his wife Isabel complained, they had not enough influence (to secure the opportunities of official employment) or, as they called it, 'interest.'[23] I dwell on these points because I think they have a bearing on Burton's subsequent development.

Burton's preoccupation with the Arab Middle East did not reflect a childhood dream, but evolved gradually from the circumstances of his early adult life. His 'desultory boyhood' – the phrase was coined by an admiring biographer of the Edwardian era – was mostly passed on the continent of Europe, at the temporary locations of his parental household. It was varied by a brutalizing year at an English boarding school. The rest of his pre-university education was what was locally available to the sons of such British expatriates of relatively high status. Lesley Blanche coyly remarks about Burton and his brother that as boys 'they had little regular education, but learned a great deal about life in such forcing-houses as Naples.'[24]

In one of his autobiographical fragments Burton – with breathtaking bravado – presents a grandiose, not to say mendacious, view of this random education that followed his father's wanderings and whims. Burton states that he went up to Oxford 'after some years of careful training for the Church /of England/ in the north and south of France, Florence, Naples, and the University of Pisa.'[25] Oxford, Burton implied, appeared to him a dim, provincial place for pedants.

In his boyhood Burton acquired a taste for learning languages, from native informants and in spoken and dialectal as well as literary forms.[26] He had an easy familiarity with French and Italian, and he was already quite widely read in the poetic and historical literature of the European Middle Ages and Renaissance.[27] His knowledge of Italian later played a part in procuring him a key appointment in his brief Indian career. Yet, as Burton himself recognized, this random continental education set him apart from his British equals and contemporaries, who could be supported and promoted by the networks of their former schoolfellows.

Oxford and the choice of India for a career

For the son of a gentleman, such an informal educational background was no bar to going up to Oxford. At Oxford Burton set out to teach himself Arabic. He describes the limited progress that he made:[28]

> Already wearying of Greek and Latin, I had attacked Arabic, and was soon well on in Erpinius's [sic] Arabic Grammar; but there was no one to teach me, so I began to teach myself, and to write the Arabic letters from left to right, instead of from right to left, i.e. the wrong way ... In those days learning Arabic at Oxford was not easy. There was a Regius Professor, but he had other occupations than to profess.

Nevertheless at this period Burton still had no irresistible 'call to the East.'[29] His principal ambition at Oxford seems to have been to thwart his father's arbitrary decision that he should take holy orders and enjoy a living in the Anglican Church. Burton achieved this by getting himself rusticated from the university. His temperament and background had disposed him to a military career, but the officer's commission that could be obtained by members of his family for him was a cadetship in the armies of the Honourable East India Company.[30] This had not been his first choice, but Burton made a virtue out of necessity:[31]

> I was asked what I intended to do, and I replied simply that I wished to go into the Army, and preferred the Indian service, as it would show me more of the world, and would give me a better chance of active service. There was no great difficulty in obtaining a commission ... My conviction is that the commission cost £500,

In view of this statement one may dismiss as routine current practice the recently published evidence that Burton and his propertied maternal aunt (through whom the commission was procured) had made statements that to the best of their belief no money had changed hands.[32]

Burton turns to oriental languages: his comments on Orientalists

When Burton terminated his university career, in his own words, he 'kept his eye steadily fixed on the main chance,' and before his departure to India he says that he 'spent all his spare time in learning Hindostani with old Duncan Forbes.[33] Elsewhere he mentions a dozen lessons with him.[34]

Forbes, though he had not passed any long time in India, was a serious and competent scholar, as well as a member of the Royal Asiatic Society. Forbes' *Hindustani and English Dictionary* provided the core of Platts' *Urdu, Classical Hindi and English Dictionary,* a work that has not been superseded today. Forbes's editions of the *Bāgh o Bahār* and other Urdu prose tales, *qissas* or *dāstāns,* with English translations and vocabularies, are models of their kind. Through his teaching of these texts, and through subsequent study under teachers in Western India, Burton was introduced to a class of tales, mostly with a strong Muslim or 'Islamicate' colouring, that had resemblances to those of the *Arabian Nights*. Burton describes Forbes with the sarcasm that he so often lavished on orientalist scholars and other rivals, but in Forbes' case Burton's habitual ferocity is mitigated by a degree of affection:[35]

A very curious old Scotchman it was. He had spent a year
or so in Bombay, and upon the strength of it, he was a
perfect master of Oriental languages. He had two passions:
one was for smoking a huge meerschaum, and the other
was for chess, concerning which he published some, at that
time, very interesting and novel studies.

Perhaps his third passion was not quite so harmless; it was
simply for not washing. He spoke all his eastern languages
with the broadest possible Scotch accent; and he cared
much more for telling anecdotes than teaching. However,
he laid a fair foundation, and my then slight studies of
Arabic secured me the old man's regard.

Burton adds, with evident approval:

He attacked Eastwick, the orientalist, in the most
ferocious style.

In later life Burton's own attacks on orientalists could also
sometimes be described as ferocious. Perhaps the most unpitying is his
dismissal of Sir William Macnaghten, editor of an early edition of the
Arabian Nights – 'Calcutta II' – but also British Envoy at Kabul during
the humiliating events of the First Afghan War. The passage also shows
Burton's schizoid approach to the rule of his fellow-countrymen over
Asian territories:[36]

McNaghten was a mere Indian civilian. Like too many of
them, he had fallen into the dodging ways of the natives,
and he distinctly deserved his death. The words used by
Akbar Khan, when he shot him, were, *'Shumā mulk-e-mā
mī gīrīd'* ('So you're the fellow who've [*sic*]) come to take
our country').

As readers of his rendering of the *Nights* will recall, Burton
displayed an especial animus against his predecessor in their translation,
the Arabist and lexicographer E.W. Lane.

Burton states that his motive for opting for service in the
Bombay Native Infantry was the fact that he had relations in the East
India Company's service in the Bengal Presidency, and he wished to
be outside their control. 'I was determined to have as much liberty as
possible, and therefore I chose Bombay.'[37]

First steps in India

Burton sailed from Greenwich in June 1842, and passed part of his time on shipboard in studying Hindostani and in 'making the three native servants who were on board talk with me.'[38] The phrase already suggests the superior and bullying manner that Burton would adopt throughout his Indian years. Burton believed that his knowledge of Hindostani was by then such that 'it enabled me to land /at Bombay/ with éclat as a griff [cadet], and to astonish the throng of palanquin bearers that jostled, pushed and pulled me at the pier, with the vivacity and nervousness of my phraseology.'[39] After disembarking at Bombay in 1842, and during his subsequent posting at Baroda, Burton's study of oriental languages proceeded under the care of Indian munshīs, professional teachers and scribes employed by British officers. Burton describes the first of these and his relationship with him after landing at Bombay:[40]

> /The Parsee manager of the army 'Sanatarium' where Burton lodged after arrival in Bombay/ recommended as *moonshee* or language master, a venerable old Parsee priest, in white hat and beard, named Dosabhai Sohrabji, at that time [1842] the best known coach in Bombay. Through his hands also generations of griffins [cadets] have passed. With him, as with all other Parsees, Gujarati was the mother tongue, but he also taught Hindostani and Persian, the latter the usual vile Indian article. He had a great reputation as a teacher, and he managed to ruin it by publishing a book of dialogues in English and these three languages, wherein he showed his perfect unfitness. He was *very* good, however, when he had no pretensions, and in his hand I soon got through the *Akhlāk-i-Hindī* and the *Totā-Kahānī* ('Tales of a Parrot'). I remained friends with the old man to the end of his days, and the master always used to quote his pupil, as a man who could learn a language running.

When Burton joined his regiment in Baroda:[41]

> Having lodged myself in what was called a bungalow, a thatched article not unlike a cowshed, and having set up the slender household, I threw myself with a kind of frenzy upon my studies. I kept up the little stock of Arabic I had acquired at Oxford, and gave some twelve hours a day to a desperate tussle with Hindostani. Two moonshees barely sufficed for me.

Around this time – apart from Hindostani – Burton embarked on the study of Gujarati ['Guzerattee'], Marathi ['Mahratti' and 'Maharatta'] and, and, according to his statements, some Sanskrit. His teachers were a Nāgar Brahman in Baroda and the regimental pandit. One must treat with suspicion Burton's repeated statements that 'eventually /his/ Hindu teacher officially allowed /him/ to wear the *Janeo* (Brahmanical thread).' If this is true, it appears to be Burton's first attempt to assume an oriental persona. After qualifying in Hindostani, in June 1843 Burton was appointed interpreter to his regiment.

The rôle of the Munshī

The munshī was an indispensable figure in the acquisition of oriental languages by any servant of the East India Company or of the British Crown in India down to the early twentieth century. The social function of the Indian munshi or teacher of languages in the British ruling community in India is caricatured with the ponderous and somewhat offensive wit of the period in G.F. Atkinson's *Curry and Rice,* first published in 1859. 'Our moonshee' is the first of the three categories of 'natives' to whom a lithographic plate with accompanying description is devoted. In the small community of 'Our Station' he takes precedence over 'Our Nuwab' and 'Our Cloth Merchants.' From Atkinson's description:[43]

> A famous Moonshee is Baghobahar![44] and a capital hand at coaching you along, and getting you through the examination, although the rascal can't speak a word of English ... If you on your part do, zealously and without interruption attend to instruction for a certain number of hours per diem, which is the usual arrangement, he on his part will undertake to infuse such an amount of Oriental knowledge into your pericranium as will enable you to emerge from the examination hall a passed man.

In this caricature Baghobahar's pupil's 'unwavering and undiverted attention is not infrequently interrupted by the intrusion of bottles of beer, soda-water and brandy.' But 'Baghobahar crosses his stockinged feet, and calculates that, with all the divergences of Dalbhat's attention,[45] also with all the hinderances [*sic*] of but little knowledge of the language having been ingrafted into him, he will still be able to coach him through.' Atkinson then describes how, for another military pupil

– 'Fudge, of the Fireeaters' – Baghobahar smuggled the answers into the examination hall with glasses of water brought in by a servant.

Burton was a keener student than this and has a kinder view of these Indian coaches than Atkinson, who was the son of James Atkinson, the early translator of Firdawsi's *Shāhnāma* and editor of the Urdu story of *Hātim Tai*. One may note that Burton often had a kinder (if equally supercilious) view of Asians than he had of his fellow countrymen.

We may list the munshīs whom Burton mentions that he subsequently employed. Burton states that he 'had not been a week in Karachi before /he/ found a language-master and a book' to teach him Sindhi;[46] but after a month or two he 'threw aside Sindī for Maharattee, hoping, by dint of reiterated examinations, to escape the place of torment (Karachi) as soon as possible.'[47] He learnt Marāthī in the summer of 1844 from the pandit who had accompanied his regiment from Baroda to Karachi. After passing in Marāthī, 'as usual in the top place' in October 1844, Burton immediately turned to Persian, for which he purchased the necessary books before he left Bombay.[48] On his return to Karachi he employed an educated Persian called Mirzā Mohammed Hosayn Shirazi. Mirzā Mohammed Hosayn was Burton's companion and teacher in Sind until he departed to Shiraz in the sunmer of 1846. We shall return later to the especial rôle that Mohammed Hosayn played in Burton's development. From him Burton gained a serious knowledge of Persian literature and of the language as spoken in Iran. Burton also spent time in the company of other Persians of high status, among them another Mirzā Hosayn, who was a brother of Āghā Khān Mahallātī, 'the first Aga Khan.'[49] According to Burton's 'little autobiography':[50]

> At the end of the first year /stationed in Sind/, when I had Persian at my fingers' ends' (and sufficient Arabic and a superficial knowledge of Panjabi) I began the systematic study of the Sindhian people, their manners and their tongue.

Burton can hardly have acquired 'Persian at his fingers' ends,' besides some Arabic and Panjabi, in the space of two months at the end of 1844, and so in this passage he must mean that he turned to Sindhi at the end of 1845. The combination of languages is the same that he mentions in another autobiographical fragment as occupying him in 1848, when he was suffering from ophthalmia. This later account is a much more specific in mentioning the munshīs whom he employed while he expanded his knowledge.[51] In the *Terminal Essay* to the *Nights,* written forty years afterwards, Burton alleged that in 1845 he was already the only officer /under Napier's command/ who could speak Sindhi, a proposition that is examined below and does not fit well with this chronology.[52]

With regard to Burton's methods of acquiring languages the testimony of a brother officer, Walter Abraham, who used to spend time in Burton's quarters in Karachi in 1847, must carry some weight, though this also was recorded more than four decades afterwards. Abraham recalls that Burton had a relay of munshīs through the day 'who relieved one another every two hours, from ten to four daily. The moonshees would read an hour and converse the next.'[53] However Abraham's testimony appears to contradict Burton's own accounts of his practice, which was to hire a munshī to embark on a new language immediately he had finished with the examination in a previous language.

When his Persian munshī Mohammad Hosayn departed to Shiraz, Burton at once engaged as an Arab coach a 'young Abyssinian' called Hājjī Jawhar, whom he took with him on his southward voyage to Goa and the Nilgiri Hills in February 1847. He evidently kept him until his return from the south towards Bombay and Karachi at the end of 1847. Burton mentions the names of his last teachers in India, at a time after his return to Sind at the end of 1847. These were Munshī Nandā, who taught him Sindhī; and Shaykh Hāshim, 'a small half Bedouin,' who continued Burton's coaching in Arabic, and taught Burton Qur'ānic recitation. Under him Burton 'began the systematic study of practical Muslim divinity' and 'became proficient in prayer, not forgetting a sympathetic study of Sufi-ism.' Burton at this time also 'when overstrung, relieved /his/ nerves with a course of Sikh religion and literature.'[54]

On the evidence of his writings, Burton learnt much more from these later teachers than he did from his earlier munshīs for Indian languages, who were those who were attached to his regiment when it was stationed at Baroda.

The walking dictionary and other Indian servants

One additional 'learning-aid' is mentioned in Burton's description of his earlier regimental life in Baroda, the 'walking dictionary' or as a later generation would say, the 'sleeping dictionary.' Such a local mistress was thought by Burton to be 'all but indispensable to the student.'[55] Burton was a man of his time, when British social attitudes hostile to the population of India were hardening with the consolidation of political

21

power. This produced a state of mind in Burton that approved the taking of Indian mistresses but deprecated the birth of children of mixed descent. Officers of his regiment, he informs us, sometimes included in the contract with their Indian female partners a stipulation that there should be no children.[56] It is perhaps not surprising that Burton thought that these Indian women seldom felt much affection for their European partners. Burton states that when he joined his regiment at Baroda in 1842, 'there was hardly an officer in Baroda who was not more or less morganatically married to a Hindi [Indian Muslim] or Hindu woman.'[57] The 18th Bombay Native Infantry, when it was posted to Sind, provoked the outrage of Sir James Simpson, the general officer commanding after the departure of Napier, at the number of Indian mistresses who accompanied its British officers.[58] Burton mentions that it was a standing joke in his regiment that one of the officers always spoke of himself in the feminine gender, because 'he had learnt all his Hindostani from his harem.'[59] This detail is matched by the testimony of a Bombay munshī of the time who mentions officers who came up for the Hindustani examination there, and would say, *Main abhī ātī hūn* – 'I'm coming now' – referring to themselves in the female gender.[60]

Finally one may note the role of Indian household servants. Burton on his voyage east in 1842 had sought out the Indian servants on shipboard in order to practise his Hindostani, and Walter Abraham also provides evidence that Burton five years later in 1847 continued to use his own domestic servants for the same purpose:[61]

> His domestic servants were – a Portuguese, with whom he spoke Portuguese and Goanese [*sic*], an African, a Persian, and a Sindi or Belochee. These spoke their mother tongue to Sir Richard as he was engaged in his studies with *moonshees*.

Abraham's judgement was clearly influenced by distant and romantic recollection and by a conviction of Burton's own manifest destiny, and one may doubt his testimony as to the degree of Burton's mastery of these spoken languages, but he writes:[62]

> It was a treat to hear Sir Richard talk; one would scarcely be able to distinguish the Englishman from a Persian, Arabian or Scindian.

British officers and oriental languages: inducements to learn

Burton was not alone among British military officers in his passion for learning oriental languages. Among others Sir Evelyn Wood, VC, [b. 1832] in his lively autobiography, entitled *From Midshipman to Field-Marshal*, testifies to a similar enthusiasm.[63] Young Lieutenant Wood had transferred from the Royal Navy to the Queen's Army. He was disappointed that he had not yet won the Victoria Cross for his heroism in the Crimea. He studied Hindustani as he sailed round the Cape in 1857, copying out the [Perso-Arabic] alphabet twenty-four times a day. On landing at Bombay, like Burton, he 'could speak a few words.'[64] In May 1858 he suffered severe sunstroke and the doctor limited his studying of Hindustani to eight hours daily.[65] Later he overtaxed his strength in endeavouring 'to read for seven hours daily with Moonshees and five to seven hours by myself.'[66] 'I was naturally fluent,' he states, 'as I took up for the examination 2000 words. /I/ had an unusual vocabulary at my command, and passed the examination for Interpreter without difficulty, at a cost of from £180 to £200.'[67] Evelyn Wood left India for good in 1860, after only two years service there at the tail-end of the Indian Insurrection. His knowledge of Hindustani was not considered any asset when he went home and applied to the Staff College:[68]

> I was questioned with immense rapidity as to my knowledge,
> being confined to a good knowledge of Hindustani and a
> slight acquaintance with French.

Forty-six years after he left India, when Field-Marshal Sir Evelyn Wood published his memoirs, he took care to put the macrons on the long vowels of Indian words.

Burton, Wood and Atkinson refer to the expenses of coaching by munshīs and their own fairly modest financial rewards on being appointed interpreters to their regiments. At the beginning of May 1843 Burton had passed first in Hindostani at Bombay, and after his return to Baroda on 26 June he was appointed interpreter to his regiment 'which added a few rupees, some thirty a month, to my income.'[69] This financial encouragement for army officers existed down to well into the twentieth century, as it did also for 'Indian civilians,' [British members of the Indian Civil Service] like StJohn Philby.[70] The present writer recalls that an uncle of his own in the Indian Army used to express his satisfaction at the fact that in the 1920s he continued to draw a salary of 50 rupees a month as Persian interpreter to his regiment through a period of active service in Burma. The structure of military interpretership examinations contributed to the high level of Persian scholarship exemplified by such early twentieth century military figures as Lieutenant-Colonel Douglas Craven Phillott, whose *Higher Persian Grammar,* characterized by Gilbert Lazard as *très riche en faits bruts,* [71] can still be consulted with profit; and Lieutenant-Colonel Sir Wolseley Haig, historian of the Deccan and Lecturer in Persian at the School of Oriental Studies in London; who was somewhat improbably the supervisor of the communist historian Kunwar Muhammad Ashraf's admirable 1930s thesis on *The Life and Conditions of the People of Hindostan, 1200-1550.* [72]

By Pattimār to Examination Hall: an Introduction to Oriental Travel

For Burton the journey to take examinations in oriental languages that were held in Bombay also afforded a lengthy and sometimes enjoyable leave from military duties. 'In those days there were no steamers up the coast,' he wrote, 'and men hired what were called *pattymārs.*'[73] These *pattimārs* were a variety of dhow with sharply raked masts, with a somewhat pear-shape bottom to the hull and a rising stern, which were in use only on the western Indian coast.[74] Early in April 1843 Burton 'considered himself thoroughly qualified to pass in Hindostani.' He 'obtained leave' from the Commander-in-Chief to visit Bombay for the purpose of examination, and found a *pattimar* to take him there from Baroda:[75]

> The sail southwards, despite the heat, was perfectly charming. The northeast monsoon, about drawing to its end, alternated with the salt sea-breeze and the spicy land-breeze ...The sky was deep blue unflecked by a single cloud, and the sea bluer ... There was perfect calm inside and outside the vessel. No posts and no parades. The living was simple enough. consisting of rice, curry and chapatis, with the never-failing tea and tobacco ... Despite landing almost every evening, the voyage down coast occupied only six or seven days.

Not all the journeys by *pattimār* to Bombay at examination times and then back to Baroda, were equally agreeable. The seas were choppy and dangerous at the break up of the monsoon, and the return journey against a prevailing northerly wind might take as long as six weeks.[76] At times Burton took a jaundiced view of the 'long list of pleasures peculiar to the pattimār.' ...'All know how by days your eyes are blinded by heat, and how by night mosquitos ... assault your defenceless limbs,' Besides this there were also musk-rats, common rats, cockchafers, fleas and lice on board.[77] Yet these coastal journeys were Burton's introduction to the conditions and pleasures of independent travel in the East, and Burton also wrote of the benefits of this 'simple way of travelling':[78]

> True, it was 'slow coach', creeping on seventy or eighty miles a day, and some days almost stationary ... The study of the little world within was most valuable to 'the young Anglo-Indian', and the slow devious course allowed landing at places rarely visited by Europeans. During my repeated trips I saw Diu, once so famous in Portuguese story, [and] Holy Dwarka, guarded outside by sharks and filled with fierce and fanatic mercenaries, and a dozen less interesting spots.

When he first joined his regiment in 1842, the servants that Burton had recruited in Bombay travelled with him on the pattimār to Bandar Tankāriya, the landing-stage for Baroda. He was similarly accompanied on later voyages.[79]

Burton's patterns of learning and examinations

When they were not active upon campaign, the routine duties of British officers in India allowed leisure for the intensive study of languages, often for eight and more hours daily, as has been described by Burton and Sir Evelyn Wood. In Burton's case, the short periods that elapsed between going up to Bombay for examination in one language and a return visit to qualify in another imply that the study was indeed intensive. Burton qualified in Hindostani on 5 May 1843 'and on May 12th I had laid in a full supply of Gujarati books, and set out by the old road to rejoin [my regiment].'[80] On August 22nd he was granted leave to go from Baroda to Bombay again to be examined 'in the Guzerattee language'. He set out from Baroda on 10 September and sat the examination on 16 October, 1843, 'again in the presence of old General Vans Kennedy and the normal three or four nobodies.' Burton again passed first. He then obtained eleven days extension of his leave to 10 November.[81]

The first of these examinations in the Town Hall in Bombay had taken Burton away from his regiment for over a month, and the second for all of two months. These prolonged absences from routine military duties may have been an additional encouragement to learn languages. The pattern matches the long leaves given to officers later in the century for *shikār* and Himalayan exploration [and implicitly for reconnaissance and espionage]; to which were added long sick-leaves granted on grounds of health, what a modern American historian of the development of Indian hill-stations has called the 'medicalization of leisure.'[82] Burton himself profited from this generosity in granting sick-leave when he went to Goa, Calicut and the Nilgiris in 1847.

Two months after his return from the examination in Gujarati his regiment received its marching orders, and in January 1844 Burton sailed with it from Gujarat to Karachi. The regiment was required for the pacification and 'settlement' of Sind following its annexation to the East India Company's territories after the successful campaign by Sir Charles Napier in 1843. The transfer from Baroda to Sind brought a decisive change in Burton's opportunities and prospects; but first we may consider Burton's continuing progress in acquiring the qualifications of military interpreter in different oriental languages.

In Sind, according to Burton's own account, the general in command, Sir Charles Napier wanted Burton to learn Sindhi through the following summer, but the project was deferred by Burton who was suffering from the intense heat:[83]

> To escape suffocation, I was obliged to cover my table with a wet cloth and pass the hot hours under it. However energy was not wanting, and the regimental *pandit* proving a good schoolmaster, I threw away Sindi for Maratha; and in October 1844, I was able to pass my examination in Maratha at the Presidency [i.e. Bombay], I coming first of half a dozen ... I at once laid in a store of Persian books, and began seriously to work at that richest and most charming of oriental languages.

According to Isabel Burton:[84]

> During those seven years in India, Richard passed in Hindostani, Guzaratee, Persian, Maharattee, Sindhee, Punjaubie, Arabic, Telugu, Pushtū (Afghan tongue), with Turkish and Armenian.

Although visits from Karachi to Bombay by steamer could be faster than they had been by *pattimār* from the Gujarat coast, there is not time in the chronology of Burton's years spent in western India for leisurely trips to Bombay to be examined in all these languages. It is also difficult to believe that the board of examiners of the Bombay Army would have regarded the study of Armenian or Telugu with enthusiasm or even complacency, and proceed to set up examinations in these languages. Other examinations were conducted locally following a general order of 27 June 1844, and the examiner's recommendations were evidently forwarded to the Board at Bombay for confirmation.[85] Burton probably made an approach to learning all these languages, and he also published 'notes on the Pushtu, or Afghan dialect' [*sic*] and claimed to be co-author with his friend Dr Stocks of a grammar of Multani, a language that is not mentioned in Isabel Burton's list. The only other examination that Burton himself mentions sitting in Bombay was in Persian. This took place three years later, in October 1847, with Burton 'coming first out of thirty', and 'receiving something more substantial, in the shape of an honorarium of Rs. 1000 from the Court of Directors'.[86]

Encounters and opportunities in the Sind Survey

When his regiment sailed for Sind, a shipboard acquaintance made after embarcation on New Year's Day 1844 aided Burton's progress. During the four days of the sea-voyage on the steamer *Semiramis* bound for Karachi, which was a small port rapidly developing under the British administration, Burton met Captain Walter Scott, a nephew of the novelist. They discovered common antiquarian and literary interests. Scott 'was delighted to meet a man who was acquainted with Froissart and Hollingshed.' More relevant to the needs of the moment, Scott had been ordered by Napier to make a survey of the canals of Sind, and he was in possession of an Italian work on the irrigation of the Lombard plain. Burton could interpret this for him. Scott brought Burton to Napier's attention and Burton was transferred from regimental to staff duties as Scott's assistant in the Sind Survey. Burton, though his aggressive temperament, high-spirited behaviour and bitter tongue brought him many enemies in later life, appears to have enjoyed an unblemished friendship with Scott. 'We never had a divergent thought, much less an unpleasant word.' Despite the vitriolic comments of Burton that we have quoted with regard to figures whom he disliked, the same is also true of some of Burton's relations with some other scholars and enthusiasts, British and continental.

The Sind Survey had been set up as an effective information-gathering organization by the conqueror Sir Charles Napier, and is an early example of the labours of the copious British governmental production of Indian 'gazetteers'. The Sind Survey was designed to harvest all kinds of conceivably useful information regarding Sind and its inhabitants. Burton was initially assistant to Scott in surveying canals and irrigation, but later was called on to write reports on a variety of topics, mainly concerned with the habits and ways of life of the local population.

A selection of the reports of the Sind Survey was published by the Bombay Government in 1855.[89] In this published selection Burton appears as the joint-author of an article on 'Division of time, articles of cultivation and modes of intoxication in Sind', and sole author of one on 'Population, Customs, Language and Literature of Sind.' The latter was 'submitted to Government' in December 1847.[90] Material from these reports was previously published by Burton himself in 1851 in his first major work, *Sind and the Races that inhabit the Valley of the Indus.* The personal journal that he must have written in these years would also have served as the basis of his first book of travels written with a more general readership in mind, *Scinde, or the Unhappy Valley.*

Disguise, rôle-playing and the ever-present Munshī

It was in Sind, on the western frontier of the Indian subcontinent, that Burton embarked upon his first prolonged explorations of oriental life, and began to make attempts to merge himself into the pattern of Muslim society, disguised in native costume. These attempts led to his adoption of the fictitious Muslim persona of al-Hājj 'Abd Allāh when he undertook his pilgrimage to Mecca and Medina. The first period of disguise in native costume dates from the time when he was gathering the materials embodied in his reports for the Sind Survey. Burton elsewhere explains his reason for disguise:[91]

> The first difficulty was to pass for an Oriental, and this was
> as necessary as it was difficult. The European official in India
> seldom, if ever, sees anything in its real light, so dense is the
> veil which the fearfulness, the duplicity, the prejudice and
> the superstitions of the natives hang before his eyes.

Burton's picturesque descriptions of the characters that he impersonated are quoted verbatim by most of his biographers. One may note the principle on which he selected his disguises, which would account for any deviation of behaviour from local practice, and for deficiencies in the spoken language:[92]

After trying several characters, the easiest to be assumed
was, I found, that of a half Arab, half Iranian, such as may
be met in thousands along the northern shore of the Persian
Gulf. The Scindians would have detected in a moment
the differences between my articulation and their own,
had I attempted to speak their vernacular dialect, but they
attributed the accent to my strange country, as naturally
as a home-bred Englishman would account for the bad
pronunciation of a foreigner calling himself partly Spanish,
partly Portuguese.

Hence Burton adopted in his early ventures the persona of Mirzā 'Abd
Allāh from Bushire, 'a vendor of fine linen, calicoes and muslins.' In
these impersonations Burton's munshī constantly accompanied and aided
him, even on his visit to the Karachi stews:[93]

My poor Moonshee was generally at hand to support me in
times of difficulty, so that the danger of being detected ...
was a very inconsiderable one.

Romantic encounters

Burton also describes his romantic encounters with the fair sex during
the course of these disguised wanderings. These descriptions appealed to
the sensibilities and curiosity of his English readers then, and continue to
be the subject of speculation today. Such excitements led to a welcome
softening of Burton's harsher attitudes towards the native population and
to the growth of his recurrent nostalgic affection for the more obviously
picturesque charms of oriental society:[94]

What scenes he saw! what adventures he went through! but
who would believe, even if he ventured to detail them?
The Mirza's [i.e.Burton's] favourite school for study was
the house of an elderly matron ... The respectable matron's
peculiar vanity was to lend a helping hand in all manner of
affaires de coeur ... So he sat upon his felt rug beneath a
shadowy tamarind ... while the soft strains of mysterious,
philosophical, transcendental Hafiz were sounded in his ear
by the other Mirza, his companion, Mohammed Hosayn
– peace be upon him!

The 'other Mirza' was of course his Persian munshī.

In this passage Burton's role appears as that of a voyeur. In his earlier volume *Scinde, or the Unhappy Valley* there is one story of his playing a more active rôle. A 'very pretty Persian girl' intrigued with Burton on the march through her 'little slave-boy', with the farcical detail of Burton sending her a bottle of sweet liqueur that he had himself concocted. The affair came to nothing, but the story may have had a factual basis.[95]

Burton takes up his pen

Before his employment in the Sind Survey, Burton had probably been in the habit of writing English verses of a rather Byronic character, and since his boyhood he had impulses to write prose treatises.[96] But from before this period of his employment in the Sind Survey we have no evidence of the sustained production by Burton of a body of descriptive writing. Contemplating Burton's vast and variegated oeuvre that followed these years in Sind, one might say that after this Burton hardly ever stopped writing. Less than two years after Burton left India, three separate works in four volumes were published in London in 1851, comprising more than 1,400 pages of print.[97] A fourth work was already in the hands of a publisher.[98] Not so much a rage to live – as Burton's most recent biographer would have it, – as a rage to get into print!

All three works published in 1851, – *Scinde, or the Unhappy Valley*, *Goa, and the Blue Mountains* and *Sind and the Races of the Valley of the Indus* – are the product of Burton's experience in the years from 1844 to 1849, when he was stationed in Sind or was sent off on sick leave. To varying degrees they reflect notes and journals kept on the spot. From internal evidence the worked-up drafts, close to the published texts, may be seen to have been completed during these years before he sailed to London in 1849.[99] Burton does not appear to have revised the two earlier books in any way that reflects the greater knowledge and more subtle outlook that he displays in the third. He wrote the books for different readerships and he may have considered that all of them would bring him money and fame without further alterations.

Scinde, or the Unhappy Valley: a work of high-spirited entertainment

Scinde, or the Unhappy Valley is clearly the earliest of these writings. Its random order of narrative and many of its descriptions are probably taken, more or less in chronological sequence, from the journal that Burton must have kept between 1844 and 1846, with some additional digressions and essays on topics that engaged his attention, inserted when he was writing up his original field-notes with a view to publication. However, he has embellished the descriptions and in general inflated his sentiments and comments on what he observed. For this he used a literary device that may have appealed to the general English public of his time, but is tedious for the modern reader. Burton pretends that he is taking a Mr Bull (i.e. John Bull, the archetypal decent no-nonsense English country gentleman) and his family on a leisurely guided tour around Sind. Comparisons are constantly made between life in Sind and life in Europe; and in the comparisons Burton draws upon the travels of his boyhood:[100]

> Here the desert is a dead flat-a horizon-bound circle of dull, hard, dry clay, like the level floor of a mud house. It bears nothing save horse and camel bones; but although there is no more grass on it than in the streets of London or Paris, a little water would soon render it verdurous as the byways of Pisa, Warwick or Arras.

In this maiden literary effort Burton's youthful remarks about the native population of Sind are fairly constantly derogatory, though he evinces an order of preferences, of likes and dislikes of particular groups. The device of explaining local conditions to Mr Bull exaggerates the strains of irascibility and facetiousness in Burton's own character. This facetiousness, characteristic of much British travel literature of this period, can be illustrated by the Chapter headings of the book:[101]

> CHAPTER XII. The Hindoos of Scinde – their Rascality and their Philoprogenitiveness.
> CHAPTER XIII. The Scindian Man – His Character and what he Drinks.
> CHAPTER XIV. The Scindian Woman – Especially her Exterior.

As might be expected Burton, prefers Middle Eastern, ethnic groups of North-Western India, and Muslims, relatively fair-skinned, as well as manly and heroic, to those who are darker-skinned, Hindu and/or engaged in the non-violent operations of commerce. I quote his description of Afghans settled in northern Sind:[102]

> These men are beyond compare the handsomest race that we have yet seen ... They yield to none in bravery and

31

rascality, and they enjoy the respect of all, as being Bacheh-Aughan, 'Sons of the Affghan' and by direct consequence, they are haughty, high-spirited and vindictive as superior race could wish to be.

In this admiring description by Burton, written probably about 1846, we see that a decade *before* the outbreak of the Sepoy Mutiny and Indian Insurrection of 1857 we see evidence of a climate of opinion that already existed, and was beginning to shape the policy of recruiting into the Indian army solely from the 'martial races' of the subcontinent. This attitude was not solely the fruit of bitter experience acquired in the years 1857-1859. It reflects an earlier shift towards a currently fashionable ideology of racial evolution and decline. Yet in spite of these sentiments Burton had no premonition or prescience of the 'Mutiny' of 1857. In the same work he expresses faith in the loyalty and fighting qualities of the East India Coy's old-style 'sepoy regiments:'[103]

There is something uncommonly grotesque in their general appearance – a total want of 'fitness of things' in an Ultra-European dress upon an Ultra-Asiatic person ... Still they are stout hearts, and true, these fellows ... you may still rely on their faith and their loyalty ... One company of them as they are is still worth half a battalion of Italians or Greeks, and when they have a few more British officers to lead them on, you may safely trust them to act against any army whatever.

The early Victorian humorous style of *Scinde, or the Unhappy Valley* is intended to give the decent English reader – 'Mr. Bull' – a comfortable sense of his own superiority. Nowadays it in fact casts a doubt on the value of Burton's evidence and judgements in this book. His judgements are usually pejorative. Eastern men are wretches, ruffians and rascals, and the women are taken to be lascivious and immoral whenever opportunity offered:[104]

The fair sex at Shikarpur has, as might be expected, earned itself an unenviable reputation.

Burton paints a discreditable picture of a new British ally, the fugitive Ismāʿīlī leader Āghā Khān Mahallātī ('the first Agha Khan'), who is said by Burton to have bastinadoed the bringer of tidings that the Baluches were about to attack his camp. The pattern of oriental despotism of the anecdote is that of Kipling's subsequent *Ballad of the King's Jest*, about alleged similar behaviour of the Amīr of Afghanistan, and has a refrain:[105]

Heart of my heart, is it meet or wise
To warn a king of his enemies?

At Jerāk in Baluchistan the Āghā Khān is said to have suffered severely for his heedlessness.[106] This anecdote told by Burton has found a place in Mihir Bose's critical biography, *The Aga Khans*.[107] But there are considerations that weigh against its veracity. It is of a recognizable recurrent pattern. Would this great survivor have behaved with such folly? Burton later became friendly with a brother of the Āghā Khān.[108]

Scinde or the Unhappy Valley is a young man's book. Isabel Burton considered it 'the freshest, most witty and spirited thing I ever read.'[109] Nowadays it is difficult to find any grounds to agree with Isabel Burton's judgement.

Goa, and the Blue Mountains: a narrative of Burton's travels in Southern India

Burton was seriously ill by the autumn of 1846, and he had evidently fallen out of grace with Sir Charles Napier and with the latter's entourage. This brought obstacles to his continuing secondment to the Sind Survey. Burton was sent to Bombay for treatment and the Surgeon General there gave him a very generous two years of sick-leave. To obtain this there is no reason to believe that he needed to resort to the pattern of malingering described in his own satirical *Anglo-Indian Glossary*, but there may have been a feeling that it was a good way to get rid of him for the time being.[110]

Burton accordingly hired a *pattimār* in Bombay and sailed in February 1847, bound for Goa, and accompanied by his favourite horse, some servants and an Arabic munshī. It is evident that he took with him the notes for the reports that he was to submit to the Sind Survey very shortly after his return there. He apparently also took with him his own manuscript translations into English of a Hindostani [Urdu) works that he had read with munshīs some years before. Burton had probably acquired a smattering of Portuguese with other Romance languages in his boyhood.and he brought with him on this journey a copy of *Os Lusiades* of Camoẽs, the Portuguese national epic that he was to translate in later years. On this trip he was able to comment on the difference of intonation of the language as spoken by the Goanese and the home Portuguese. Among the other books that he had on board was a *Historical Sketch of Goa* by the Abbé Cottineau de Kloguen.[111]

Burton's illness did not prevent him spending six weeks sightseeing in Goa and then looking round the ports of Ponani and Calicut, before he went up to the hill-stations of the Nilgiris, where he was meant to recuperate. The two small volumes of the previous work, *Scinde or the Unhappy Valley,* are conservative in format for their time. When Burton set out on his sick-leave, he gathered material for a different and more up-to-date kind of travel book with illustrations. As a boy Burton had taken drawing lessons in Italy, and he could provide the lithographers with sketched views and even human figures of some competence and charm.[112] Although in *Goa, and the Blue Mountains* the lithographs were not yet coloured, he thus set the pattern for the subsequent illustrated popular narratives of his travels, the *Pilgrimage to El-Medinah and Mekka* (1855) and *First Footsteps in Africa* (1856).

Burton's style also became less sententious. Exeunt the tedious Mr. Bull and family. In his new book Burton himself was also more truly a tourist traveller on this South Indian trip, with no large stake in the country and society that he was recording; and he padded out his account with useful 'guidebook' information – such details as the price of accommodation in Ootacamund or of commodities in Calicut. What he observed in Calicut was later to afford material for speculative annotations in his translation of *Os Lusiadas* to the passages of Camoẽs describing Vasco da Gama's landfall there. Burton's descriptions of the buildings and landscape are commonplace, but his comments on Goanese society are of some value as a historical record of the time in which they were written, when other English descriptions are sparse. Occasionally the contrast between Goa and British India gave him food for thought, and he speculated that the the condition of Portugal might one day 'doom their now worse than useless colony to form part of her payment of debts,' which would lead the Portuguese to hand over Goa to the British.[113]

Burton believed that those of mixed race were inferior to both of their parents, and he dwelt on this theme in *Goa, and the Blue Mountains*. In his opinion, 'neither British nor Portuguese India ever produced a half-caste at all deserving of being ranked in the typical order of man.'[114] Goanese Muslims were few but superior.[115] Even the local Hindus had an advantage: 'The men generally surpass in strength the present descendants of the Portuguese heroes.'[116] The situation and attitudes of the *mestiço* population of Goa provoked him to thought:[117]

It is sufficiently amusing to hear a young gentleman whose appearance, manners and colour fit him admirably to become a bandboy to some Sepoy corps, talk of visiting Bombay, with letters of introduction to the Governor and Commander-in-chief ... Yet at the same time it is hard for a man who speaks a little English, French, Latin, and Portuguese to become the lower clerk of an office on the paltry pay of 70*l.* per annum ... No wonder that the black Portuguese is an utter radical.

One chapter reflects an enduring interest of Burton. He and two other Englishman had read a romanticizing account of a village or small town populated by dancing-girls in the Goa territories, and they decided to visit the settlement. From Panjim [New Goa, Panaji] they went up the Zuari creek by canoe to Seroda [Siruda], a village where they found about twenty establishments, and a total number of 50 or 60 dancing-girls, though some more were away from the settlement, 'engaged at Panjim, or the towns round about.' 'There is hardly a second-rate station in the Bombay Presidency that does not contain prettier women and as good singers.' The dancers were 'common-looking Maharatta women,' but 'the verses were in Hindostanee and Portuguese, so that the performers understood as much as our young ladies when they perform Italian bravura songs.' Included in this chapter is the tale that we shall examine below of an old English infantry officer who had fallen in love with a dancing girl, and had come to live his last years here. [120]

In *Goa, and the Blue Mountains* the information regarding Calicut and Malabar, whither Burton sailed from Goa, is mainly derivative and of little relevance to his development as an orientalist The same may be said of his descriptions of the hill stations of Coonoor and Ootacamund and of British society there, which fill the latter part of the volume. But we may note that this portion of the book also describes Burton's encounters with the Todas of the Nilgiri Hills. Burton made and included in the book a well-drawn and evocative sketch of these curly-headed tribals against the rolling background of the Nilgiri plateau. Passages of his narrative at this point in some respects anticipate Burton's later descriptions of travel in tribal societies in Africa.

The 'boxed stories' in *Goa, and the Blue Mountains*

Burton may have felt that his previous composition, *Scinde or the Unhappy Valley* with its single story of the 'very pretty Persian girl' was short on romantic interest. Three stories of romantic love have been inserted in Burton's description of Goa, at points where one suspects that their purpose is to enliven the narrative. They are told as true stories, and in an assessment of Burton's veracity as a witness the evidence of these stories must surely have some weight.

The first boxed story is of a dying Jogi who was sitting beneath a tree by the Strada Direita of Old Goa, where Burton, who had been wandering around in the moonlight, was led to talk to him. 'He told us the old story, the cause of half the asceticism in the East – a disappointment in an *affaire de Coeur*.' The man was a Maratha trooper of the British, who had fallen in love with a Brahman widow and carried her off from her husband's funeral pyre. But as the two were riding away an archer loosed an arrow and wounded her mortally. The horseman carried her body and buried it beneath the tree where he was sitting, and he himself turned Jogi. The day after Burton saw him the Jogi died.[122]

The story does not explain why trooper carried the body away from his 'native hamlet in the Maharatta hills' and put it down at the end of the Strada Direita in Old Goa. The answer must be that Burton felt that in this romantic location he needed a story like this to accompany 'the soft whisperings of the night breeze' that 'alternately rose and fell with the voice of the waters.[123]

A longer boxed story is supposedly narrated by Burton's Goanese servant about an earlier British employer.[124] The Sahib was a Lieutenant, who had visited Goa about ten years back. He gained admission to the convent of Santa Monaca [Monica] in Old Goa, with the intention of abducting 'a very pretty white girl' who taught Latin there. The Sahib and 'an Affghan scoundrel' who was in his employ entered the convent at dead of night when the guards had been drugged, apparently by the pretty white girl, but the men went to the wrong room and carried off the Sub-Prioress. They only discovered their mistake when they looked at their prize outside the walls of the convent:[125]

> But imagine /the Sahib's/ horror and disgust when, instead
> of the expected large black eyes and the pretty little rose-
> bud mouth, a pair of rolling yellow balls glared fearfully
> in his face, and two big black lips, at first shut with terror,
> began to shout and abuse him with all their might.

Burton depicts the Sahib very much as he would have liked others to see him. The servant is given a name like that of Burton's own Muslim servant. Burton in a half-joking fashion clearly wished the hero of the story to be identified as himself, but he used the narrative frame as a disclaimer if he should be accused of relating a lying fiction. The story is of an anecdotal pattern which is too *ben trovato* to be true. Given its setting in a Roman Catholic convent, one should perhaps search for its analogues in the Italian collections of stories that Burton had known since he was a boy. Elements of it are found in several tales of Boccacio's *Decameron*.[126] However the touch about the negroid face of the Sub-Prioress reflects another of Burton's own obsessions.[127]

A weak point in the tale is that Burton does not explain why the sleeping lady was carried out of the convent without a murmur, and only outside its walls does she begin to shriek and scold them. The descriptions of the Sahib who is the hero of the story – allegedly from the tongue of the Goanese butler – show, in the high colours of romantic fiction, the rôle into which Burton was now coming to project himself, the 'ruffian' Sahib who could take on a full variety of personae in different religious and cultural systems, but was predominantly attracted towards Muslim society and its usages: [128]

> He was a very clever gentleman, who knew everything. He could talk to each man of a multitude in his own language, and all of them would be equally surprised by, and delighted with him. Besides his faith was every man's faith. In a certain Mussulmanee country he married a girl, and divorced her a week afterwards. Moreover he chaunted the Koran, and the circumcised dogs considered him a kind of saint. The Hindoos also respected him, because he always eat [*sic*] his beef in secret.

The Sahib impressed the Jews and the Parsees equally. 'At last my master came to Goa, where of course he became so pious a Christian that he kept a priest in his house to perfect his Portuguese.' Later, when he penetrated the convent accompanied by his 'Affghan scoundrel' who is made to tell the tale:[129]

> 'My master's face – as usual when he went upon such expeditions – was blackened, and with all respect, speaking in your presence, I never saw an English gentleman look more like a Mussulman thief.'

Readers may recognize the fantasy as a less attractive adult variant of Kipling's Kim as 'Little Friend of all the World.'[130] In their adult life some other British Indian military figures have been credited, with the same charisma.[131] In the frame of the story Burton has made use of the mischievous narrative device of the double-cross, in which the narrator makes a statement that is not untrue [*viz.* that the anecdote is not about himself], but tells the story in such a way that his hearers or readers will discount the disclaimer. Burton's niece, Miss Stisted, and following her other biographers, have been taken in by this and have believed that it was a true story about Burton himself.

The last boxed story in *Goa, and the Blue Mountains* is of the old British officer of Native Infantry (the branch of the army of the East India Company to which Burton belonged), who came to the village of Seroda to many the nautch-girl whom he loved.[133]

She would never marry him unless he would retire from the service to live and die with her in her native town.

The tomb was pointed out to Burton and he reflected:

It is always a melancholy spectacle, the last resting-place of a
fellow-countryman in some remote nook of a foreign land.

This last boxed story is interesting as a fantasy expressed by Burton of absorption into a Hindu, not a Muslim environment. In his lush portrayal of this environment, with similes derived from English translations of Sanskrit literature, the descriptions anticipate Burton's other work in a Hinduizing vein, his pseudo-translation *Vikram and the Vampire*.[134] The sentiments seem to be borrowed by Burton as an exercise in a genre, rather than entered into with the heartfelt enthusiasm that he displays in his harsher Islamicate fantasies.[135] Both the tale of the Jogi in the moonlight in Old Goa and that of the British officer and the dancing girl bear some resemblance to the romantic tales, some of them written by C Meadows Taylor, that appeared in Bacon's *Oriental Annual* in the years 1837-1840.[136] The tales in the *Oriental Annual* were accompanied by steel engravings of the ruins against which they were set, to which Burton's own lithographic sketch of the churches of Old Goa forms a parallel.[137]

The texts of Fort William College, and the limits of Burton's Hindu learning at this time

When he sailed southward from Bombay, Burton had evidently brought material to work upon, including his reports for the Sind Survey.[138] To this material he turned in his enforced leisure at Ootacamund. Another possible fruit of Burton's leisure during his months of sick leave is the autograph manuscript of a collection of oriental tales that was formerly in the library of the Royal Anthropological Society in London, and is now in the Huntington Library in California. The manuscript is a closely written fair copy with a mock-up title page bearing the place and date 'Bombay ... 1847.'[139] It is clear that this inscription indicates a project to print the work from this copy, and does not refer to the date and place of the completion of the manuscript. Apart from the scurrilous juvenilia circulated at Oxford, this is the earliest evidence that we possess of Burton's desire to appear as a published author.

Burton titled his translation AKLAQ I HINDI, with the sub-title 'A Translation of the Hindūstānī Version of Pīlpāy's Fables.' The *Akhlāq-i Hindī* is indeed a version of the *Pancatantra* stories, though with a different frame story from that of Bīdpāī/Pīlpāy. The *Akhlāq-i Hindī* derives from Visnūśarman's *Hitopadeśa*, via the *Mufarrih al-qulūb* ['The Delighter of Hearts'), which is a free adaptation in Indianized Persian dating from the early sixteenth century. The Urdu/Hindostani text was commissioned by Dr Gilchrist from Mir Bahadur 'Ali, one of the munshīs of Fort William College, Calcutta, and was printed in Calcutta in 1803. [140] As noted above, Burton read the *Akhlāq-i Hindī* with his first munshī when he landed in Bombay in 1842.[141] Excerpts from the *Akhlāq-i Hindī* were on the curricula of Hindostani examinations for British officers even in the twentieth century .

In *Goa, and the Blue Mountains* there is a statement about the Hindu learning of the matron [madam] of the house where Burton spent the night that sheds light on the knowledge of Indian literature that Burton then possessed:[142]

> Our Matron was powerful at reciting Sanscrit shlokas (stanzas), and, as regards Pracrit, she had studied all the best known works, as the 'Panja Tantra' together with the legends of Vikram, Rajah Bhoj, and other celebrated characters.

The modern student of indology may gasp at Burton's youthful belief that 'the Panja Tantra' [sic] was in Prakrit The references that he then makes to Vikram and Raja Bhoj, are to two cycles of tales, to the *Simhāsanadvitrimśataka* or 'Thirty-two Tales of the Lion-Throne' – and to the *Vetālapancavimśati* or 'Twenty-five Tales of a *Vetāla* ['undead being']'. The latter cycle Burton freely adapted under the title *Vikram and the Vampire*. Burton's adaptation was not published till 1870, but this a text that Burton had read either with Forbes or at a later date with one or other of his Hindostani munshīs in western India. The work is referred to in the preface of 1870 edition by its Hindostani title of *Baitāl pachīsī*.[143] This is another indication that what Burton had before him was the Fort William College Hindostani version, which was published in verbally near-identical Urdu (Perso-Arabic script) and Hindi (Devanāgarī script) printings shortly after 1801.[144]

Before he left India in 1849 Burton was certainly no Sanskritist, though the Nāgar Brahman at Baroda and the regimental pandit may have taught him rudiments of grammar. His familiarity with Sanskritic Indian literature was mainly confined to the vernacular prose versions compiled at Fort William College around 1801, for the benefit of young British servants of the East India Company.

Burton's reading of these Fort William College texts during his seven years in India, often in the presence of munshīs whose rôle we have studied, was not without unpredictable benefits. It strengthened a taste for tales of wonder that had been formed by his wide reading in older continental European literatures, a taste that had been nurtured in his boyhood accompanying his parents on their European wanderings and by his early education 'on the continent without system.' His boyhood reading evidently also included Galland's version of the *Nights* in French or English translation. In *Scinde or the unhappy Valley* he refers to 'those dear old frenchified *Arabian Nights*.'[145] A lifelong predilection towards such tales, sustained by the study of these vernacular south Asian collections of tales during his years of Indian service, ultimately bore fruit in Burton's massive annotated translation of the *Arabian Nights*.

Burton's return to Sind

Burton cut to seven months the two years of sick leave that he had been given. Four months of the rains had been spent in the Nilgiris, where he contracted the 'rheumatic ophthalmia' which debilitated and incapacitated him up till his departure from India two years later.[146] Though he had taken an Arabic, not a Persian coach, with him to the Nilgiris, he still felt sufficient confidence to sit the examination in Persian in Bombay in October 1847, in which he passed out top. He then returned to active service, rejoining the Sind Survey.[147] Shortly after his return, on 31 December 1847 he 'submitted to Government' the first of his two official reports, *Notes relative to the population of Sind, and the customs, language and literature of the people*. His second report (written in collaboration with Surgeon J.E.

Stocks), *Remarks on the division of time, and the modes of intoxication in Sind,* followed three months later in March 1848.[148]

Sindh, and the Races that inhabit the Valley of the Indus: a Gazetteer

The Sind Survey reports can be closely linked with the third of Burton's works published in 1851, *Sindh and the races that inhabit the Valley of the Indus.* It was the most serious, and is nowadays the most readable of the early books from Burton's Indian years. This is in part because it was written for a different class of readers. Like the reports that Burton had 'submitted to Government' – which published them four years later in 1855 – *Sindh and the Races that inhabit the Valley of the Indus* is conceived as an official publication. and its printing was subsidized by what Burton – possibly with tongue in cheek – described as 'the liberal patronage which the Court of Directors of the Hon. E.I. Company have ever been ready to extend to their servants.'

The book as an avowedly official work of record, a kind of social gazetteer of the province of Sind, laid constraints upon Burton's writing that were almost wholly beneficial. Burton was free to express his opinions, and there are numerous touches and turns of phrase reflecting his individual style and views. But Burton was under an obligation both to stick to the truth and to stick to the point. He also no longer had to entertain a class of unspecialized readers among the early Victorian public, and to indulge them with reflections embodying sentiments about an alien land and its British conquerors of a kind that they would approve. There is no more of Mr. Bull and his family, and there is much less of pejorative turns of phrase about natives and 'niggers' that were habitual in Burton's writing and disturb modern readers. It is noteworthy that of Burton's works *Sindh and the Races that inhabit the Valley of the Indus* has been reprinted in Pakistan, where sections of public opinion are particularly sensitive. The format also discouraged Burton from lengthy disquisitions that stray from the main theme of the narrative.

Some of the matter of the book is shared with *Scinde or the Unhappy Valley,* but it is differently treated. As an example we may take the story of the seven headless corpses which is found in both works. The seven corpses jointly fill the role of Nostradamus in prophesying the course of future events in pithy verses. In *Scinde or the Unhappy Valley* the tale is turned into an English ballad stanza:

41

For years to come broad Ar shall flow,
But when it dries by Fate's decree,
The fierce Beloch shall sell his son
For silver pieces two and three.

By contrast *Sindh, and the Races that inhabit the Valley of the Indus* reproduces the two lines of the original Sindhi text, accompanied by a literal translation:

1. Long and long shall the Ar remain full of water, but when at last it shall dry up;
2. In those days the children of the Beloch shall be cheap and valueless in the land.

As was the case in the two other works published in the same year (1851) Burton was not inclined to revise his text. Hence in *Sindh, and the Races that inhabit the Valley of the Indus* inconsistencies are visible between different parts of the book, reflecting the fact that Burton's knowledge was derived or copied from a variety of sources. For instance the passages in Sindhi that Burton reproduced were very carefully transliterated with such features as superscript short vowels. On the other hand Arabic and Persian words were much more casually transcribed, seldom marking the '*ayn* guttural and with vowels corresponding to his teacher Mirza Mohammed Hosayn's Shirazi pronunciation.

From internal evidence much of the information contained in *Sindh and the Races that inhabit the Valley of the Indus* was gathered in the last two years that Burton passed in India; that is, if we accept the internally consistent account of the order in which Burton extended his studies and employed his munshīs, and match this with the contents and order of the work. Other sections of the work appear to have been reorganized in the same period. This late date is perhaps surprising as Burton refers to his frequent incapacitation by eye-trouble at this time.[154] The task of compilation required single-mindedness, powers of concentration and industry. From a literary as well as from a scholarly point of view *Sindh and the Races that inhabit the Valley of the Indus* is much the most valuable of the literary works produced by Burton in his formative years in India. Burton began with accounts of the province's history and topography, where he admits that he has drawn upon earlier writers. As might be expected from his earliest tasks under Walter Scott, he described irrigation and the related subject of taxation. Then follow chapters on language and literary culture, mostly filled by a lively account of 'the most important and best known of the popular legends of our province' illustrated by poetic quotations.[155] The next chapter is on traditional education, while Chapter VIII deals with 'the present state of society in Sind.' It discusses matrimony, and here Burton refers to a work, said to be in Sindhi, on 'The Lawful Pleasures of Women'. This is followed by 'Intoxication, and the different preparations in use,' in which information was re-used from the paper that Burton submitted in the Survey. The chapter concludes with a copious account of 'the occult sciences,' a subject that continued to evoke Burton's interest through his life.[156] He next gives an account of *tasawwuf* or Sufism, which is of value for its descriptions of *dhikr* and similar Sufi practices based on personal observation and initiation. Burton is also exceptional in his time in perceiving *tasawwuf* as potentially a 'formidable political engine'.[157] The further chapters of the book, which include descriptions of 'the Stranger Tribes' settled in Sindh and of the Sindhi Hindus, are of equal value.

Burton had produced a classic descriptive work of its period, which stands comparison with Lane's *Account of the Manners and Customs of the Modern Egyptians* (1836) and is superior in many ways to the *Qanoon-e Islam* of Herklots [1832], two slightly earlier models with which Burton was familiar.

Eyes set upon Mecca: Burton at the end of his Indian training

The man who wrote *Sindh and the Races that inhabit the Valley of the Indus* had gathered and organized a vast body of information, from personal observation, from reading and from enquiry. He seems to have advanced far beyond the young officer who had passed interpretership exams by cramming of Fort William College texts with munshīs. He had now acquired linguistic skills, a fund of knowledge regarding the behaviour of individuals in Islamic society and a skill in rôle-playing that impelled him towards the climacteric of his life, the journey to Mecca.

Burton had no cause for modesty at this achievement, and, given his character, it was not to be expected that he would exercise this virtue. Indeed, freed from the restraints of a demi-official publication, the old Adam, or old Burton, reasserts himself and he ventures on some very shaky ground in stating his claims and his ambitions at the end of the course of study that filled his Indian years: [158]

> It was always my desire to visit Meccah during the pilgrimage season ... So to this preparation I devoted all my time and energy; not forgetting a sympathetic study of Sufi-

ism, the *Gnosticism* of Al-Islam, which would raise me high above the rank of a mere Moslem. I conscientiously went through the *chillā* [sic], or quarantine of fasting and other exercises, which, by-the-by, proved rather over-exciting to the brain. At times, when overstrung, I relieved my nerves with a course of Sikh religion and literature: the good old priest solemnly initiated me in the presence of the swinging *Granth,* or Nanā Shāh's Scripture. [By Nanā Shāh Burton meant Gurū Nānak! - SD] As I had already been invested by a strict Hindu with the *Janeo* or 'Brahminical thread', my experience of Eastern faiths became phenomenal, and I became a Master-Sufi.

A Terminal Note on the *Terminal Essay* of the *Nights*

The dates that Burton mentions when he states that he was engaged in studying particular languages involve us in a curious problem of chronology. His two surviving official reports were only submitted in 1847, the year of Sir Charles Napier's departure from Sind. According to his fragmentary autobiographies, Burton 'threw aside Sindi for Maharatti' only a month or two after landing at Karachi in January 1844. On June 27th [of the same year] there was a general order establishing a vernacular examination [in Sindhī], 'making it every officer's duty to learn something more or less of the language.'[160] No teacher for Sindhi is mentioned by him by name before Munshī Nanda in 1848.[161]

In Burton's account in the *Terminal Essay,* written some 40 years later, he claims that he was [already] in 1845 'the only British officer who could speak Sindi,' and it was for this reason that he was asked by Napier to submit his report on 'lupanars or bordels, in which not women but boys and eunuchs lay for hire.' Burton refers to what he wrote as 'my unfortunate official' /report/ and says that 'it found its way to Bombay with sundry other reports.'[162] These 'other reports' are identified by Burton himself in a footnote as the two papers submitted in December 1847 and March 1848. It is at least curious that Burton submitted no other reports, either cited in this passage or referred to elsewhere, in the intervening period of two years after 1845, the year in which he alleged that he was engaged by Napier to compile the report on the brothels.

Other details of this description also provoke thought. What Burton here describes as the 'townlet of two thousand souls' of Karachi is said to have   supported no less than three of these 'lupanars or bordellos'.[163] This contrasts with the more modest number of seven aged female go-betweens resident in Karachi, four Muslim and three Hindu, whose profession was to undermine the virtue of married women. [164] Burton also says that he himself had opened no less than three shops in this small town, where he sat in disguise to observe the vagaries of native life (and apparently remained unrecognized in the confined area of the 'townlet').

When Burton visited Goa, as we have noted above, he went to a village famous for its 'dancing-girls' and found that there were not more than 20 establishments and 50 or 60 women in residence.[165] This ratio suggests that perhaps there might have been not more than three or four inmates in each of the 'lupanars or bordellos' of Karachi. They may have been places of infamy, but hardly of lavish entertainment.

Burton states:[166]

Accompanied by a Munshi, Mirza Mohammed Hosayn of Shiraz, and habited as a merchant, Mirza Abdullah the Bushiri (i.e. Burton himself) passed many an evening in the townlet, visited all the porneia and obtained the fullest details which were duly despatched to Government House.

It is also unlikely that Burton's munshī, a Shirazi, would have picked up more than a smattering of Sindhi. As for Mirza 'Abdullāh from Bushire [Burton in his oriental disguise], who was able to converse in the *linguae francae* of Persian, Arabic and Hindostani, such a man in the multilingual societies of the ports and trading posts of South Asia and the Persian Gulf would not have been expected to communicate in fluent Sindhi when he visited a brothel. The reason given for Napier deputing Burton to this peculiar task is invalid. There is no independent testimony to the existence of this earlier report and no copy of it has ever surfaced. Was its existence a figment of Burton's imagination? [167]

NOTES

1 Somadeva, *Kathāsaritsāgara,* tr. C.H. Tawney. Edited with introduction, fresh explanatory notes and terminal essay by N. M. Penzer, 10 Vols., London: 1924-1928.

2 F Lacôte, *Essai sur Gunādhya et la Brhatkathā,* Paris 1908, pp. 173-8; J.A.B. van Buitenen, *Tales of Ancient India,* 1961, reprint New York 1982, pp. 202-40. The transmission is not through the Prakrit *Vāsudevahindī* of Sanghadīsa, where the cognate name [Sānudāsa] of the hero of the epic is lost; *Vāsudevahindī,* ed. Caturvijaya Muni and Punyavijaya Muni, reprint Gandhinagar 1989, pp. 126-56; see also Moti Chandra. *Trade and trade routes in ancient India,* New Delhi 1977, pp. 129-37.

3 Van Buitenen, op. cit, pp. 231-3; R.F. Burton, tr., *The Book of the Thousand Nights and a Night,* 'Benares'/London, 1885-8; reprinted Burton Club, 15 Vols., [1906], VI. pp. 74-7. Henceforth cited as *Nights.*

4 Mss: Ethé, IO, 788-792; Ivanow, ASB, 318[2] [I8c., Indian paper]; Rieu, BM. 764B [India, 17th century]; Digby Acc. 81, ff. 40-70. The last Ms has a colophon dated 7 Dhī Hijja, 27th year of Awrangzeb's reign/27 November 1683 at Bijapur.

5 Eastern Turkish, see Ethé, IO, p. 521, composed in 960/1553; Dakanī, see note 7 below; Pashto, *mathnavī* by Sayyid Rāhat Allāh, *Sayf al-mulūk,* Miyān Hājī Muhammad 'Abd al-Khāliq, Fazal Malik. Bāzār Qissa-khwānī, Peshawur [pre-1959] and another shorter poem, with the same publisher. A popular tradition links the name of Prince Sayf al-Mulūk to a lake high above the Khāgān valley in northern Pakistan. For a Sindhi version, see Burton, *Sindh and the Races that inhabit the Valley of the Indus,* p. 135. The editor of the Dakanī version by Ghawwāsī (see n. 8 below) mentions a [19th-century Urdu] 'drama' by Akhtar Sahāranpūrī, published by Sant Singh in Lahore; Ghawwāsī, op.cit., intro., p. 20.

6 See *Nights,* X. pp. 499-500, 522; Anon., *The Persian and Turkish Tales from the French of M. Pétis de la Croix,* London 1809, pp. 302-27.

7 Ghawwāsī, *Mathnavī-yi Sayf al-Mulūk u Badī' al-Jamāl,* ed. Mir Sa'ādat 'Alī Razavī, Silsila-i Yūsufiyya No.6, [Hyderabad Deccan] 1357 Faslī.

8 I would suggest that there may be a late medieval Indian original underlying the plot of the tale of Sayf al-Mulūk, in which near the outset of his wanderings the hero is in thrall to a dark African princess but eventually finds his fair aerial princess. This is an allegorical structure intended to depict the progress of the soul that is found in Avadhī Sufi *premākhyāns*. For this structure a date much earlier than the fifteenth century is unlikely, cf. the plots of Malik Muhammad Jayasī, *Padumāvati* and Usmān, *Citrāvali*. See also Aditya Behl, *Rasa and Romance: an Indian Islamic Literary Tradition, 1379-1545*,(forthcoming).

9 Robert Irwin, *The Arabian Nights: a Companion*, London 1994, p.22.

10 For the complete edition cited see note 3 above.

11 Isabel Burton, *The Life of Captain Sir Richard F. Burton*, 2 Vols., London 1893 (hereafter cited as *Life*); Georgina M. Stisted, *The True Life of Capt. Sir Richard Burton*, London 1896. Burton's own narratives of the events of his early life are mostly found in three different fragments of autobiography that are reproduced verbatim in his wife's *Life*.

12 M. Lovell, *A Rage to Live*, London 1998.

13 Fawn M. Brodie, *The Devil Drives*, London 1967; Penguin 1971.

14 Byron Farwell, *Burton: a Biography of Sir Richard Burton*, London 1963.

15 Lesley Blanch, *The Wilder Shores of Love*, London 1954.

16 *Life*, I, p. 162.

17 Burton, *Nights*, X, pp. 205-6; Lovell, *A Rage to Live*, p. 816, n. 33 states that 'several scholars ... doubt that it ever existed.' My own doubts are mainly based on the difficulty of reconciling Burton's brief account of the assignment with the chronology of his Indian studies, see the Terminal Note to this paper.

18 Kipling was sacked by George Allen, the chief proprietor of *The Pioneer* newspaper at Allahabad. Kipling himself states that he was given six months' pay in lieu of notice; *Something of Myself*, London 1937, p. 75. The circumstances in which, at the end of 1888, Kipling was probably persuaded to leave India, are briefly described [evidently from oral tradition, with a coded reference to 'a sour-faced captain called Hearsey', i.e. Andrew Hearsey, who had been called by Kipling 'a brown Captain'] in Lord Birkenhead, *Rudyard Kipling*, London 1978, p. 90. More details of the legal manoeuvrings that Kipling's remarks provoked are given in Zoe Yalland, *Boxwallahs: the British in Cawnpore, 1857-1901*, Norwich 1994, pp. 328-30. The incident evidently delayed Allen's knighthood by some years; cf. *Something of Myself*, p. 73; C Carrington,

Rudyard Kipling: his life and work, London 1955, p. 51n. The tradition that Allen also made *The Pioneer* 'pay his passage for a trip abroad [to England via Japan and the United States] in return for articles,' suggests that Allen may have felt that it was desirable that Kipling should not be available as a witness in possible actions in the Calcutta or Allahabad High Courts; cf. Angus Wilson, *The Strange Ride of Rudyard Kipling*, London 1977, p. 119.

19 Burton, *Life*, I. p. 159.

20 C E Buckland, *Dictionary of Indian Biography*, London 1906, p. 64, s. v.

21 Blanch, *The Wilder Shores of Love*, p. 19.

22 W M Thackeray, *Vanity Fair*, OUP 1983, p. 109.

23 Cf. R F Burton in *Life*, I, p. 163.

24 Blanch, *The Wilder Shores of Love*, p. 21.

25 *Life*, I, pp. 152-3.

26 *Life*, I, pp. 81, 83.

27 *Life*, I, pp. 126,153.

28 *Life*, 1, p. 77.

29 Burton wrote in his 'little autobiography' of 1852:

After begging the paternal authority in vain for the Austrian service, the Swiss Guards at Naples and even the Légion étrangère, I determined to leave Oxford coûte qui[*sic*] coûte. *Life*, I, p. 153.

30 *Life*, I, pp. 88,92, 153. With the casualties of the First Afghan War there were hopes in the minds of Burton and other young officers of swift promotion in Indian service; *Life*, pp. 99, 153. For hopes of promotion arising from the death of senior officers on active service, cf. B Farwell, *For Queen and country*, London 1981, p. 56; cf. also the toast in army messes 'a bloody war and a sickly season', quoted in V Kiernan, *European Empires from Conquest to Collapse, 1815-1960*, Fontana 1982, pp. 25, 45.

31 *Life*, I. p. 92. One must dismiss as misleading Burton's statement in his 'Little. Autobiography' that it was his father who 'provided /him/ with a commission In the Indian army,' *Life*, I. p. 153.

32 Lovell, *A Rage to Live*, p. 25. Lovell gives credence to this statement. The sum that Burton later alleged had changed hands, £500, appears plausible. Around 1840, in the Queen's army, in which commissions were purchased on an approved and regulated basis, the base rate for the purchase of an ensign's commission in an undistinguished regiment of the line was £450, and the actual purchase money that changed hands often much more than this; see B. Farwell, *For Queen and Country*, London 1981, p. 58. The prohibition of purchase-money for nominations to the

E.I. Coy's service was evidently often tacitly ignored, particularly when Directors had assigned the nominations to their friends; cf. the remarks of young officer as to the 'sacrifice' of his family when a deed was signed in 1852 procuring his entry into the East India Coy's army, quoted in P Stanley, *White Mutiny: British Military Culture in India 1825 – 1875*, London 1998, p. 30.

33 *Life*, I, p. 93.

34 Burton in the 'Little Autobiography'; *Life*, I, p. 155. This early curriculum vitae, written around 1852, is at places a less credible account than the other two later autobiographical fragments that Isabel Burton reproduces; cf. notes 29 and 31 above. I

35 *Life*, I, pp. 93-4. Burton's notice of Duncan Forbes is, as in other cases, not entirely accurate. Forbes had spent not 'one year or so in Bombay' but three years in Calcutta; see Buckland, *Dictionary of Indian Biography*, p. 149. s. v. English accusations of a lack of hygiene among Scots were common after the Jacobite invasion of 1745. Such jibes of the English against the Scots were exacerbated by the Gordon Riots of 1783 in London and even travelled east; cf. Cantonese export plates of c. 1785 illustrating the popular song 'Sauney in the Bog-House'; David S Howard, *A Tale of Three Cities: Canton, Shanghai & Hongkong*, London, Sotheby's, n.d. c. 1996, pp. 120-1, Fig. 148.)

E.B. Eastwick (1814 – 1883 was seven years older than Burton. Burton had good cause to envy his comfortable and interesting career. Eastwick like Burton had served in a Bombay Native Infantry Regiment, and had shown a similar application in learning oriental languages. This had attracted the attention of H.H. Wilson and procured his appointment as Professor of Hindustani at the East India Coy's College at Haileybury. Of his numerous translations from Persian, Hindostani and Hindi, that of Kāshifī's *Anwār-i Suhaylī* ('Lights of Canopus,' a Persian adaptation of the *Hitopadeśa*) is perhaps the best known, and it has not been superseded. Eastwick's more tractable personality meant that academic honours and favourable diplomatic postings came more easily to him than to Burton. He was elected FRS and FSA, and was called to the Bar. He served as Secretary of Legation at Teheran, as a Member of Parliament, and as Private Secretary to Lord Cranborne (the future Earl of Shaftesbury) when the latter was Secretary of State for India; see Buckland, *Dictionary of Indian Biography*, s.v.

Sir W.H. Macnaghten was also a rival 'orientalist', and Burton also had cause to envy the advantages to which he was born.

His father Sir William Macnaghten (1793-1841) was, a Judge of the Supreme Courts of Madras and Calcutta, who like his son had attained a Baronetcy W.H. Macnaghten went to Madras in the East India Company's army, but was taken into the Governor's Bodyguard, and was then transferred to the Bengal Civil Service. He began to gain prizes for his mastery of Oriental languages and 'gained great distinction in languages at Fort William.' He rose to importance when he became adviser on their dealings with Asian power-holders to two Governors General in succession – Lord William Bentinck and Lord Auckland – and became 'Secretary to the Secret and Political Departments'. Macnaghten, arrogant in his manner towards those whom he did not consider his social equals and to Asians in general, excited the admiration of the Governor-General Lord Auckland and the latter's vivacious sister the Hon. Emily Eden. Macnaghten was the main planner of the policy which resulted in the humiliations and disasters to the British of the First Afghan War. While still in Kabul he was appointed Governor of Bombay but was unable to leave before he was killed in the deteriorating local situation which he had done much to provoke; see Buckland, *Dictionary of Indian Biography*, s.v. Buckland has no mention of Macnaghten's considerable scholarly achievement, an edition of the Arabic text of the Arabian Nights (*Alif layla*), 4 vols. printed in Calcutta, 1839-42. This has been described as 'the fourth and last of the historically important printed versions of the *Arabian Nights* ... Hence it was chosen by Torrens, Payne, Burton and Littman as the basis for their translations;' Irwin, *The Arabian Nights: a Companion*, pp. 44-5.

36 *Life*, I. p. 95. However Akbar Khān's words were not spoken to Macnaghten who as 'Envoy and Minister at the Afghan Court of Shah Shuja' went to parley with this Afghan prince and other leaders. Akbar Khān had personally dragged the envoy head-first downhill from the conference they were holding, but his manner of death was not witnessed by any British observer. It is unlikely that Macnaghten was, as Burton states, shot by Akbar Khān himself. It is more likely that he died from the sword-cuts of a surrounding mob over whose actions Akbar Khān had limited control. After this had occurred, the remark that Burton quotes was made by Akbar Khān to another of the British negotiators. This was Colin Mackenzie (afterwards Lieutenant-General Sir Colin Mackenzie), whose life Akbar Khān had just saved from attacks by infuriated Ghāzīs, while Mackenzie was riding pillion behind him; see P. Macrory, *Kabul*

catastrophe; the retreat of 1842, Oxford 1986, p. 195.

37 *Life*, I, p. 95.

38 *Life*, I, p. 98. In the 'Little Autobiography' Burton also refers to lessons 'from a native servant on board the *John Knox*'; *Life*, I, p. 154.

39 *Life*, I, p. 154. Perhaps the true and jocular meaning of this sentence, which would have been understood by contemporary readers, is that Burton had already memorized some word of *gālī* (abuse in Hindostani) of the kind that were usually acquired by all classes of the British who served in India.

40 *Life*, I, p. 101; cf. I, p. 131. In the latter description Lovell misunderstands Burton's phrase 'a venerable Parsee, named Dosabhai Sohrabjee, also a mūbid or priest, as his white cap and coat showed.' Lovell takes this to mean that Burton employed two munshīs in Bombay, cf. *A Rage to Live*, p. 29. According to the 'Little Autobiography', after landing in Bombay he spent his first evening in India in the company of Dosabhai Sohrabjee; *Life*, I, p. 154.

41 *Life*, I, 107-8.

42 *Life*, I, pp. 122-3. Lovell's speculations about ceremonies of Brahmanical initiation are hypothetical. A Nāgar Brāhman of Gujarat is not a 'Snake Priest'; cf. *A Rage to Live*, p. 39. Nāgar Brāhmans are a prominent sub-caste who derive their name from the town of Vadnagar; see A.K. Forbes, *Rās Māla*, ed. H G Rawlinson, O U P 1927, II, 234, 258.

43 [G.F. Atkinson], *'Curry & Rice'on forty plates: or the ingredients of social life at 'Our Station' in India*, London [1859], Plate 22, text unpaginated.

44 The comic name Baghobahar (*Bāgh o bahār* –'The Garden and Springtime') is taken from the title (incorporating an *abjad* chronogram of the date of composition) of *The Tale of Four Darwesh* by Mīr Amman, the best-known of all the Hindostani stories commissioned for British cadets at Fort William College, Calcutta. *Bāgh o bahār* attained the widest circulation of all the 'vernacular' works commissioned for the study of East India Coy cadets and writers studying at Fort William College, and exercised a significant influence in the growth and diffusion of Hindostani/Urdu prose, and Mīr Amman's introductory account of the growth of the language at the *Urdū-i mu'allā*, the imperial Mughal camp or court, while somewhat misleading, has been largely responsible for the prevalence of the name of Urdu, by which the language is known today. It was a text about which one can say that almost every British

learner of the language read with his munshī. Burton's teacher Duncan Forbes produced a very competent edition of the text with vocabulary and translation, which was in great demand; London 1846, with 'New and Corrected' editions in 1849 and 1862. Burton's rival Eastwick (see note 35 above,) also made a 'literal translation' (1851). Other translations of the *Bāgh o bahār* seem to have been prompted by its rôle as a work of literature or entertainment. Major Lewis Ferdinand Smith made a translation 'from the Oordoo tongue of Meer Ummun of Dhailee', which was published in Calcutta in 1813, with reprints in Bombay in 1841, and in Delhi in 1970. A lively translation in an 'Indian Variety of English' by Muhammad Zakir was published by Penguin books, India in 1994. There is an exhaustive modern critical edition of the Urdu text edited by Rashīd Ahmad Khān; New Delhi, Anjuman-i Taraqqī-i Urdū (Hind), 1992, 2nd printing 1999, 710pp.

Of these translators Lewis Ferdinand Smith had an eventful career. On the title page he claims to have been 'late secretary to his Majesty's embassy to Persia.' He was a military adventurer mainly in the service of the Marāthas under the command of de Boigne and Perron. He campaigned against George Thomas of Hansi, and with the troops of the Begam Samrū against a pretender called Sultān Shāh, who claimed to be 'Abd al-Qādir Rohila (who blinded the Mughal emperor Shāh 'Ālam II) lately returned from Mekka. Smith's writings, mainly published in Calcutta journals, deserve to be collected; see H. Compton, *A particular account of the European Military Adventurers of Hindustan*, London 1893, pp. 398-400.

45 Dalbhat (*dālbhāt*), Atkinson's humorous name for the British officer learning Hindostani, means 'lentils and rice'. The names of all those depicted by Atkinson are meant to be humorous. To savour their humour requires a superficial knowledge of the Hindostani that the munshīs imparted to civil and military officers of the Raj. 'Other ranks' ('gorahs', literally 'palefaces', British common soldiers) and memsahibs also 'picked up' a less grammatical version of this *bāt* or *bolī* ('vernacular speech') without the assistance of munshīs.

46 *Life*, I, p. 154.

47 *Life*, I, p. 155.

48 *Life*, I, p. 143; cf. pp. 129, 155. Burton furnishes no information as to how he bought grammars and oriental texts in Bombay. One publication clearly intended for army officers who were candidates for examination in Bombay is Moonshee Nizam-ud-deen's Hindostani translation of

Aesop's Fables, published in 1850, 'revised and approved by the late Major General Vans Kennedy', to whom Burton has referred in his account of the examinations in Bombay This text was, according to the title page, 'Printed at the Duftur Ashkara Press For Ibrahim Futta Mahomed and sold by him at Meadow Street below Mr. Cannon's Library.' Burton also praises lithographic printing [in Arabic script] as one of the circumstances 'fast preparing a royal road for the Oriental learner'; *Goa, and the Blue Mountains*, London 1851, p. 152. Burton evidently purchased some of the fine lithographed printings produced by Shirazi scribes in Bombay during this period. 'An excellent and correct lithograph of Mirkhond's celebrated history, the 'Rawzat el Safa', may now be bought for 3*l*. or 4*l*.[pounds sterling]; a few years ago the student would probably have paid 70*l*. or 80*l*. for a portion of the same work in the correct MS;' loc.cit. The lithographed edition of *Rawzat al-Safā* was first printed in Bombay in 1845; Storey No. 123, *Persian Literature*, I, Pt I, p. 95. Burton's idea of the price of manuscripts is probably exaggerated, as in the early nineteenth century (and until a few decades ago) Persian historical manuscripts were sold in London by the book auctioneers Sotheby and the early nineteenth-century booksellers Howell and Stewart for a few guineas each; prices and catalogue cuttings are preserved in volumes acquired by Sir Thomas Phillipps. Items from the large scholarly collection of Persian manuscripts formed by A.G. Ellis were offered for even less in 1946; see Luzac, *Bibliotheca Orientalis*, xlv, London 1945, pp. 3, 35.

49 *Life*, L pp. 144, 145. Lovell confuses the latter with Burton's munshī Mirzā Mohammad Hosayn Shīrāzī; *A Rage to Live*, pp. 47-8. Both of these figures left for Iran and shortly afterwards lost their lives there. The latter died of cholera at home in Shiraz, while the former was taken prisoner by the Shāh and brought to Tehran, 'lashed to a gun carriage'; *Life*, I, pp. 145, 155.

50 *Life*,I, p.155.

51 *Life*, I, p. 150. According to Isabel Burton this account was written in 1888; *Life*, I, p. 130.

52 *Nights*, X, p. 205.

53 Walter Abraham in a letter to the editor of *The Times of India*, dated October 31, 1891; quoted in *Life*, I, pp. 182-3.

54 *Life*, I, p. 150.

55 *Life*, I, p. 135.

56 *Life*, I, p. 109. 'Some even stipulated that there were to be no

children.' Burton's statement may imply that there was a recorded marriage contract of a Muslim type, perhaps similar to that of temporary *mut'a* marriages among Shi'īs; see *Shorter Encyclopaedia of Islam*, s.v. *mut'a*. However the negotiations may have been purely verbal. They suggest the presence of a Chaudharayan or Matron of an organized household of *Tawā'if*, capable of negotiating favourable terms for the long-term support of a suitable girl by a British officer; cf. Hasan Shāh, *Nashtar*, tr. Qurratulayn Hyder, *The Nautch Girl*, New Delhi 1992; V T Oldenburg, 'Lifestyle as resistance; the case of the courtezans of Lucknow' in V Greff, ed., *Lucknow: memories of a city*, New Delhi 1997, pp. 136-54.

Burton's detestation of the offspring of racially mixed unions (the expression of which in his *Goa, and the Blue Mauntains* is discussed below) is extended to the children of his brother officers in the Karachi cantonment:

> ...another bungalow, jealously trellised round with bamboo-work, a gaudy palanquin lying near the dirty huts, and two or three jaunty, debauched-looking 'darkies', dressed in the height of black dandyism, show manifest traces of the 'Booboo.'
>
> *Scinde or the Unhappy Valley*, I, p, 39.

Among nineteenth century Anglo-Indian writers Burton seems to be alone in referring to Indian female partners as 'Booboos', contrasted with 'Beebees', the latter term most curiously used by him to refer only to white women. This peculiar usage by Burton (unattested elsewhere, cf. *Hobson-Jobson*, s. v. BEEBEE, p. 78) has been taken from Burton by Dr Mildred Archer in her own writings from the 1960s onwards, and nowadays sometimes occurs in popular discussions of the subject in the media of the UK.

57 *Life*, 1, p. 108.

58 A letter on this topic by General Sir James Simpson is reproduced in Lovell, *A Rage to Live*, p. 73.

59 *Life*, 1, p. 109.

60 Moonshee Nizam-ud-deen, *Aesop's Fables*, Bombay 1850, Intro., p. 14.

61 Walter Abraham in the letter quoted in *Life*, I, pp. 182-3.

62 Abraham in loc. cit. H T Lambrick commented à propos of Burton's alleged linguistic facility:

> Despite the instances one comes across in romantic novels

about India, of the British officer whose Pushtu, or Urdu, or other local language was 'indistinguishable' from the tongue as spoken by the country people, or again the 'old hand' who could 'pass as a native' – persons with more than superficial experience in one or other Indian provinces know that in practice this did not happen. During my own time Sindhi friends used to tell me that they knew of only one Englishman ... whom they might mistake for one of themselves if they heard him taking part in a Sindhi conversation behind a curtain.

> Richard F Burton, *Sindh and the Races that inhabit the Valley of the Indus*, Karachi reprint 1973, H T Lambrick's intro., p. xii.

One may compare Burton's own remarks about earlier Britons who had acquired such linguistic expertise:

> The Macnaghtens, the Burneses, and generally those who devoted their time and energies, and who prided themselves most on their conversancy with native dialects and native character, are precisely the persons who have been the most egregiously, the most fatally, outwitted and deceived by the natives.

> *Scinde or the Unhappy Valley*, London 1851, II, p. 3.

Ironically Burton's remarks are applicable to his own handling of affairs during his tenure of the consulate at Damascus in 1869-71. This was a potent factor in ensuring that Burton never again got a Middle Eastern consular posting.

Lambrick's remark about romantic novels seem to apply particularly to the prolific production of Maud Diver. A mid-twentieth century example would be Berkeley Mather's *The White Dacoit* (London 1974). A sub-category of these popular narratives is of the tales of the adventures of European children lost in India who speak the language fluently, of which Kipling's *Kim* is the prime example and Sarah Jeannette Duncan's *Sonny Sahib* is also an appealing tale, perhaps suitable reading for rich foreigners on luxury tours of the palaces of Rajasthan; see also Simon Digby, '*Tulsipur Fair*, or the Boy Missionary: a Model for Kipling's *Kim*', *Indian International Centre Quarterly,* New Delhi, Spring 1998, pp. 106-25.

63 Sir Evelyn Wood, VC, *From Midshipman to Field-Marshal*, London 1906, reprint 1914.

64 *From Midshipman to Field-Marshal*, p. 88. Cf. Burton's description of himself landing in Bombay, *Life*, I, p. 154, quoted above, and note 39 above.

65 *From Midshipman to Field-Marshal*, p. 90.

66 *From Midshipman to Field-Marshal*, p. 113.

67 *From Midshipman to Field-Marshal*, pp. 115-16.

68 *From Midshipman to Field-Marshal*, p. 137.

69 *Life*, I, p. 123.

70 P. Knightley, *Philby, KGB Masterspy*, London 1988, p. 24. Between 1911 and 1915 StJohn Philby is stated to have received Rs.10,000 in cash payments from government for passing examinations in Indian languages, at a time when, owing to official disapproval of his conduct of a case, he received no increments in salary in the Indian Civil Service. The financial inducements for passing examinations in Indian languages were important to impecunious army officers, among them Generals Sir William Robertson and Sir Ian Hamilton; see Farwell, *For Queen and Country*, p.60.

Perhaps some attention should be turned to the psychological traits of British officers serving in the East that have led some of them rather than others to devote attention to the acquisition Indian and other oriental languages. A conspicuous devotion to their military profession is visible in Field-Marshals Slim and Auchinleck (see note 131 below). Among American soldiers the parallel of General 'Vinegar Joe' Stilwell may be noted. Already an excellent linguist, Stilwell by his own strongly expressed wish became the first American army language officer for China in 1919; Barbara W.Tuchman, *Stilwell and the American experience in China, 1911-45*, New York 1970, p. 61 and passim.

StJohn Philby and Richard Burton, besides their pro-Arab enthusiasm shared a strain of reckless disregard for the sensibilities of others and the likely consequences of their courses of action. One may also recall that both StJohn Philby and another 'orientalizer', Major Francis Yeats-Brown were detained by the British government in the Second World War as vocal sympathizers with Adolf Hitler. An historical link that should perhaps be noted here is that when the Burton medal of the Royal Asiatic Society was instituted StJohn Philby was the first of my predecessors to receive the award.

71 Lieut-Col. D.C. Phillott, *Higher Persian Grammar for the Use of the Calcutta University, showing differences between Afghan and modern Persian, with notes on rhetoric*, Calcutta 1919, royal 8vo, 927pp.;

G.Lazard, *La langue des plus anciens monuments de la prose persane*, Paris 1963, p. 19, n. 36.

72 K.M. Ashraf, 'The Life and Conditions of the People of Hindostan, 1200 – 1550, *Journal of the Asiatic Society of Bengal*, 1935; Letters, pp. 103-359; reprinted Delhi 1959; 'K M Ashraf on himself,' in Horst Kruger, ed., *Kunwar Muhammad Ashraf; an Indian scholar and revolutionary,1903-1962*, Delhi, People's Publishing House, 1969, pp. 396-7. Among the unpredictable links of Anglo-Oriental society, Wolseley Haig was acquainted with the eccentric Maharaja of Alwar, patron of the young Ashraf.

73 *Life*, I p. 105.

74 On the *pattimār*, see Clifford W Hawkins, *The Dhow; an Illustrated History of the Dhow and its World*, Lymington 1977, pp. 106-9, and plates on pp. 108, 109; cf. H Yule and A C Burnell, *Hobson-Jobson*, London 1903, s.v. PATTAMAR, p. 687.

75 *Life* , I, p. 120.

76 *Life*, I, pp. 105,124.

77 *Goa, and the Blue Mountains*, London 1851, p. 3.

78 *Life*, I, pp. 132-3. Diu is off-course west and Dwarka even further from the sailing route between Bombay and Tankāriya Bandar, mentioned by Burton as the landing-stage for Baroda. However sailing in the *pattimārs* the northward voyage was the more difficult. 'As the winds were generally northerly these tubs often took six weeks over what a civilized craft now does in four days;' *Life*, I, p. 105. Burton also mentions that his first northward voyage from Bombay took a fortnight; loc.cit. He makes clear that he visited Diu and Dwarka on one of his northward voyages, as he states, 'the end of the trip was Tankária Bunder:' *Life*, 1, p. 133. The *pattimār* must therefore have reached Dwarka when it was tacking against the North wind. Burton's concluding sentence mentions 'a dozen other less interesting places' which would imply that the *pattimārs* also cast anchor at such roadsteads in Kathiawar as Porbandar, Mangrol, Verawal or Gogha.

Tankāriya Bandar lay on the mud flats of the northern side of the estuary of the Dhadhar river as it discharged into the Gulf of Cambay. Called Tankārī, it is characterized as no more than a 'fishing port or boat-haven' in Mughal times; I Habib, *An Atlas of the Mughal empire*, Delhi, Oxford University Press, 1982, Map 7B and commentary, p. 25. Evidently larger vessels than the ordinary *pattimār* could moor there in the 1840s, as Burton states that his whole regiment embarked there 'in a native craft' for Bombay in December 1843; *Life*, I, p. 143. If this statement is true, it must have been a 'native craft' of exceptional size.

79 *Life*, I, p. 148; *Goa, and the Blue Mountains*, p. 15, 306.

80 *Life*, I, p. 137; cf. note 48 for Burton's purchases of books in Bombay.

81 *Life*, I, p. 124.

82 Dane Kennedy, *The Magic Mountains; Hill Stations and the British Raj*, Delhi 1996, p. 31.

83 *Life*, I, p. 143.

84 *Life*, I, p.159.

85 *Life*, I, pp. 129, 151. In the latter passage Burton mentions his examination in Panjabi conducted locally. Cf. *A Rage to Live*, pp. 157-8 for the procedure. Lovell there relates the subsequent disaster of Burton's examination in Arabic at Aden, which finds no mention in Isabel Burton's *Life*.

86 *Life*, 1, p. 149.

87 *Life*, I, p. 126.

88 *Life*, I, p. 140.

89 *Selections from the records of the Bombay Government*, No. XVII, New Series, ed. R Hughes Thomas, Bombay 1855; reprinted as *Memoirs on Sind*, 2 Vols., Delhi 1993.

90 *Memoirs on Sind*, pp. 613-636,637-658.

91 Burton's 'little autobiography' in *Life*, I, p. 155; *Falconry in the Valley of the Indus*, London 1852, quoted by Lambrick in his introduction to the Pakistani reprint of *Sind and the Races that inhabit the Valley of the Indus*, Karachi 1973, p. xiii.

92 *Life*, I, pp. 155-6.

93 *Life* , I, p. 156; cf. *Nights*, X, pp. 205-6.

94 *Life* , I, p. 157.

95 *Scinde or the Unhappy Valley*, I, pp. 72-80.

96 Cf. Brodie, *The Devil Drives*, p. 39; Lovell, *A Rage to Live*, p. 22.

97 (1) *Scinde or the Unhappy Valley*, (2) *Goa, and the Blue Mountains; or, Six Months of Sick Leave*, (3) *Sind and the Races of the Valley of the Indus*. The second of these appears to be the earliest printing, as Burton is mentioned as its author on the title page of both other works. There was a second printing of *Scinde or the Unhappy Valley* before the end of 1851.

98 *Falconry in the Valley of the Indus*, London 1852; cf. *Life*, I, pp. 158-9.

99 This conflicts with the impression given by Isabel Burton, that the papers compiled in 1848-9 'were all preparatory to becoming an author;' *Life*, I, p. 158.

100 *Scinde or the Unhappy Valley*, II, p. 279.

101 *Scinde or the Unhappy Valley*, I, p. viii.

102 *Scinde or the Unhappy Valley*, II, pp. 276-77.

103 *Scinde or the Unhappy Valley*, I, pp. 42-3.

104 *Scinde or the Unhappy Valley*, II, p. 275.

105 Rudyard Kipling, *Poetical Works*, Wordsworth 1994, pp. 247-50.

106 *Scinde or the Unhappy Valley*, I, pp. 190-6.

107 Quoted in Mihir Bose, *The Aga Khans,* Kingswood 1984, pp. 39-40.

108 *Life*, I, p. 145. One may see a similar trajectory in the literary oeuvre of other British exoticists ('orientalists'in the terminology of the late Edward Said). Once more there is a parallel of the youthful Burton with the young Rudyard Kipling, the cub-reporter of *The Civil and Military Gazette* and author of *Plain Tales from the Hills*;(cf. also notes 18 and 167). An initial mocking knowingness about 'oriental nature' is a strategy aimed at securing the attention and approval of the dominant British military and colonial service peer-group whom both Kipling and Burton approached from situations of relative social disadvantage. After readership and reputation has been secured for each of these popular and widely read elucidatory writers based on his own supposed especial inside knowledge or insight, derogation of their own especial exotic 'other' will have the effect of diminishing, in the eyes of the peer-group whom he cultivates and serves, both their status as informants and the perceived value of their special knowledge or powers of perception. In both Burton and Kipling this situation may have been a factor in the apparent growth of a more affectionate approach to these special subjects in their more mature and widely-read works. The same rhythms can also be observed in the trajectories of some modern interpreters of the exotic 'other'.

109 *Life*, I, p. 158.

110 Lovell, *A Rage to Live*, p. 78; cf. *Goa, and the Blue Mountains*, p. 4; and *Life*, I, p. 148, where Burton attributes the grant of two years' leave to 'the assistance of my friend Henry J Carter.'

111 Revd Denis L. Cottineau de Kloguen, *An Historical Sketch of Goa*, Madras 1831, reprinted Bombay 1910 and Madras 1988. Burton's text reads 'de Kleguen'; *Goa and the Blue Mountains*, pp. 44, 69.

112 Burton as a boy had taken drawing and painting lessons at Naples

and at Pisa, and was aware of the problems of illustrating books from drawings taken on the spot; *Life*, I, pp. 49,60-1. 'I have been able to make my own drawings, to illustrate my own books. Travellers who bring home a few scrawls and place them in the hands of a professional illustrator, have the pleasure of seeing the illustrated paper style applied to the scenery and the people of Central Africa and Central Asia and Europe. Even when the drawings are carefully done by the traveller-artist, it is hard to persuade the professional to preserve their peculiarities'; *op. cit.* p. 61. The example that he then gave, of a drawing from Sind sent to England, suggests that he was preparing illustrations for *Scinde, or the Unhappy Valley*, which were not included in the publication.

113 *Goa, and the Blue Mountains*, p. 100.

114 *Goa, and the Blue Mountains*, p. 157.

115 *Goa, and the Blue Mountains*, pp. 106.

116 *Goa, and the Blue Mountains*, p. 107.

117 *Goa, and the Blue Mountains*, p. 101.

118 *Goa, and the Blue Mountains*, p. 124.

119 *Goa, and the Blue Mountains*, p.I23.

120 *Goa, and the Blue Mountains*, pp. 127-32.

121 *Goa, and the Blue Mountains*, plate facing p. 339.

122 *Goa, and the Blue Mountains*, pp. 63-8.

123 *Goa, and the Blue Mountains*, p. 63.

124 *Goa, and the Blue Mountains*, pp. 73-89.

125 *Goa, and the Blue Mountains*, p. 84.

126 There are analogues to the separate elements of Burton's tale of the attempted rescue from the convent at Goa in several of the 'novels' of Boccacio's *Decameron*: a beautiful foreign damsel immured in a convent in a faraway land, cf. 2nd day, Novel VII; and the explanation by his daughter given to the Soldan of Babylon of her adventures, (tr. J M Rigg, London, Everymen's Library, 1930, I, p. 118); the entry of the hero into the convent for purposes of seduction, cf. 3rd Day, Novel I, 'Masetto da Lamporecchio feigns to be dumb, and obtains a gardener's place at a convent of women, who with one accord make haste to lie with him,' (I, p.155); involvement of a senior nun in the story, ibid., (I, 160); and 9th Day, Novel II, 'an abbess rises in haste, intent to surprise an accused nun,'(II, pp.232-4]; cf. also 1st Day, Novel IV, an abbot shares the favours of a girl brought in by a young monk, (I, pp.38-9): kidnap over a castle wall, with escape by a waiting ship; cf. 2nd Day, Novel IV, the Soldan of Babylon's daughter, taken by the Duke of Athens from the castle of the

Prince of Clarenza, I, p. 110).)

127 Cf. Robert Irwin, *The Arabian Nights: a Companion*, pp. 33-4.

128 *Goa, and the Blue Mountains*, pp. 73-4.

129 *Goa, and the Blue Mountains*, p. 82.

130 Rudyard Kipling, *Kim*, London 1891, p. 4:
   His nickname through all the wards was 'Little Friend of
   all the World.'

131 Perhaps the latest example is Field-Marshal Sir Claude Auchinleck, with his ability to converse in Pushto, Panjabi and Hindostani; Philip Warner, *Auchinleck: the lonely soldier*, London 1982, pp. 17-18. Field-Marshall Slim records an occasion in 1943 when he himself was addressing troops and passed from speaking Hindostani into Nepali without being conscious of the change; Sir William Slim, *Defeat into Victory*, London 1957, p. 189.

132 *Goa, and the Blue Mountains*, pp. 127-30.

133 *Goa, and the Blue Mountains*, p. 130.

134 Richard F Burton, *Vikram and the Vampire, or Tales of Hindu Devilry*, London 1870; cf. note 143 below.

135 Cf. Burton's later judgement in his comparison of the contents of Somadeva's *Kathāsaritsāgara* ('*The Ocean of Story*', tr. C H Tawney) with the *Arabian Nights* [*Nights*, X, pp.160-1, note 2]:
   And finally there is something in the atmosphere of these
   tales, which is unfamiliar to the West and which makes them,
   as more than one has remarked to me, very hard reading.

136 Thomas Bacon, *Oriental Annual, containing a Series of Tales, Legends and Historical Romances*, London 1840, frontispiece and plate facing p. 2 of Penukonda, with accompanying legend 'Penkonda', (evidently contributed by C.Meadows Taylor), pp. 1-24. Cf. *Goa, and the Blue Mountains*, plate facing p. 60. In the same volume of the *Oriental Annual* was an article on the 'Neilgherries.' This spelling was adopted by Burton, and one suspects that a copy of the volume may have been available to him at a public library in Ootacamund. However the spelling is common to other descriptions of the period, e.g. Captain Walter Campbell, *The Old Forest Ranger, or, Wild Sports of India in the Neilgherries* [etc.], London 1842.

137 *Goa, and the Blue Mountains*, plate facing p. 339.

138 *Nights*, X, p. 206, note 2. The date suggests that Burton complied with a deadline immediately after his return to Sind.

139 Farwell, *Burton*, p.46 reproduces a sketch for the layout of the title

page; Brodie, *The Devil Drives*, p.80, note; Lovell, *A Rage to Live*, p. 815, n. 17.

140 Mir Bahādur 'Ali Husayni, *Akhlāq-i Hindī*, Calcutta 1803; *Akhlak i Hindi or Indian Ethics*, ed. with introduction and notes by Syed Abdoollah, London 1868.

141 *Life*, I, p. 131.

142 *Goa, and the Blue Mountains* , p. 125.

143 *Vikram and the Vampire or Tales of Hindu Devilry*, London 1893, reprint Delhi 1985, Preface to the First (1870) edition, p. xvii. Confusion has been created by Burton's own disingenuous presentation of this work:

> It is not pretended that the words of these Hindu tales are preserved to the letter ... I have ventured to remedy the conciseness of their language and to clothe the skeleton with flesh and blood; op. cit., p. xxxi.

By my own count less than 5 percent of Burton's text of *Vikram and the Vampire* is identifiable translation from the Fort William College text of *Baitāl pachīsī*. This is fleshed out by Burton into a fantasy in Hindu Mode, which works in the results of note-taking from English works including W Ward's *View of the Hindoos* and the early volumes of *Asiatic Researches* of the Bengal Asiatic Society. The information is ill-digested and awkwardly inserted to give spurious local colour to the narratives. It may well reflect the contents of a notebook from Burton's first years in India.

Verbal similarities in those sentences distinguishable as actual translation suggest that Burton made use of an untraced early nineteenth century printing of an anonymous English version of the *Baitāl pachīsī* that has been reprinted as *Stories of Vikramaditya (Vetala Panchavimsati)*, Bombay, Bhavan's Book University, 1960.

144 Gyan Chand, *Urdū kī natharī dāstānen*, Karachi 1969, p. 668; R B Saksena, *A history of Urdu literature*, Allahabad 1940, p. 250. For a sketch of the early Sanskrit recensions of the *Vetālapañcaviṁśati* cycle see Śivadāsa, tr. C. Rajan, *The Five-and-twenty Tales of the Genie*, Penguin, New Delhi 1995, pp. xiii-xiv. The Fort William College Urdu and Devanāgarī script versions by Lallūji Lāl and Mirzā Lutf 'Alī 'Wilā', apparently working in collaboration, are said to derive from an early eighteenth century version in Braj Bhākhā [sic] by Sorath Kabīshwar, commissioned by Maharaja Savā'ī Jay Singh of Amber/Jaypur in the reign of the Mughal emperor Muhammad Shāh (1719-1748). Names of characters in the tales have been updated to those fashionable in the later

Mughal period and are so reproduced by Burton. Burton's selection of 11 tales correspond with the versions of *Baitāl Pachīsī* as follows: 1 = 1; 2 = 4; 3 = 3; 4 = 9; 5 = 13; 6 = 2; 8 =- 14; 9 = 5 combined with 6; 10 = 10; 11 = 25. Tale 7 is an invention of Burton, for which there is no basis in the text.

The existence of the sketched layout for a title page in his autograph manuscript of his English manuscript translation of *Akhlāq-i Hindī* dated '1847' suggests that Burton may also have made an early draft for *Vikram and the Vampire* during his Indian years.

145 *Scinde or the Unhappy Valley*, II, p. 217.

146 *Life*, I, pp. 148-9.

147 Lovell, *A Rage to Live*, p. 82.

148 *Nights*, X, p. 206, n. 2; Richard F Burton, *Sindh and the Races that inhabit the Valley of the Indus*, with an Introduction by H T Lambrick, Karachi 1973, pp. vii-viii; Life, I, p. 158.

149 *Sindh and the Races that inhabit the Valley of the Indus, with Notices of the Topography and History of the Province*, London 1851, Preface p. vi; Karachi 1993 reprint, p. xxii.

150 See note 147 above. The edition was published in Oxford in Asia Historical Reprints, Karachi, Oxford University Press, 1993.

151 *Scinde or the Unhappy Valley*, II, p.167.

152 *Sindh and the Races that inhabit the Valley of the Indus*, p. 89.

153 *Life*, I, pp.150, 151.

154 *Life*, I pp. 148, 149, 150, 151.

155 *Sindh and the Races that inhabit the Valley of the Indus*, p. 89.

156 Magical works, e.g. that of Zadkiel, were part of Burton's informal reading at Oxford; *Life*, I, p.155; cf. also *Goa, and the Blue Mountains*, pp. 128-9. The interest is evident in his notes to the *Nights*.

157 *Sindh and the Races that inhabit the Valley of the Indus*, pp. 203-4.

158 *Life*, I, p. 150

159 *Life*, I, pp. 154-5.

160 *Life*, I, p. 129.

161 *Life*, L p.150. The munshī 'Mr Hari Chand, a portly, pulpy Hindoo', described at some length and with evident distaste by Burton, was not in Burton's own employment. He was a political go-between and negotiator, later employed by Āghā Khān Mahallatī; *Scinde or the Unhappy Valley*, II, pp. 131-9.

162 *Nights*, X, pp.205-6 and note.

163 *Nights*, X, p.205. Elsewhere Burton states that Karachi 'now [i.e.

in 1849-51?] contains about 24,000 inhabitants, and the large military cantonment adds every day population and prosperity to the place;' *Sindh and the Races that inhabit the Valley of the Indus*, p. 5. Other estimates for the total population of Karachi immediately before the British annexation usually approximate to 14,000, but with many of these living outside the walls; A F Baillie, *Kurrachee, Past Present and future*, Calcutta 1890, pp. 28-30. It is clear that Burton's 'townlet' refers to the 'old town' or 'native town' within the ramparts, of which a sketch from c. 1830, a map of 1838, and later traces remain. The ramparts are a quadrangle of about 400-500 yards on each face; Baillie, op. cit., map facing p. 52; Y. and M.H Lari, *The Dual City: Karachi during the Raj*, Karachi 1996, pp. 34, 76, 157; cf. *Scinde, or the Unhappy Valley*, I, pp. 28-9. In a census of 1889 the Old Town Quarter had a population of 7,552 living in the fort area of 30 acres. It was considered extremely congested; Lari, op. cit., pp. 157-8. Allowing for increased congestion, Burton's estimate of 2,000 appears too low, and not improbably should be doubled. A town of modest size is still indicated by these figures.

164 *Sindh and the Races that inhabit the Valley of the Indus*, p. 297.

165 *Goa, and the Blue Mountains*, p. 124.

166 *Nights*, X. p. 206.

167 Numerous studies of the political history of the twentieth century, a period when an abundance of contemporary documents has been preserved, show how divergent and unreliable the memories of the participants and sufferers in events tend to be, especially when they are recorded decades afterwards. Bad faith need not always be presumed, for the processes of recall, influenced by repeated rehearsal and narration, themselves distort the narrative to what would better suit the narrator.

Perhaps another parallel to that we have previously made (see notes 18, 109) can be adduced between Kipling and Burton in the delusive operations of long-term memory. Kipling in his autobiography, written in old age, refers to 'a really filthy job, an inquiry into the percentages of lepers among the butchers who supply beef and mutton to the European community of Lahore;' *Something of Myself*, London 1937, pp. 44-5. As the editor of Kipling's early pieces of journalism remarks, 'If he actually wrote such a thing, it has not been found;' see Thomas Pinney, ed., *Kipling's India: Uncollected Sketches 1884-88*, London 1986, p. 69.

I suggest that the occasion which is likely to have been transformed by the operations of Kipling's memory was his visit to the cowsheds and gullies of the cattle-keepers of Lahore. At the time – more than half a century earlier – he wrote a long and hair-raising description, which he defended from charges of exaggeration, of the sources of the city of Lahore's milk-supply, and the cows which 'often give milk to the *Sahib-logues*' [sic]; Pinney, pp. 69-77. There is no mention of lepers, let alone the calculation of the percentage of them in the local population.

INDEX